Organic
Gardening

ORGANIC
GARDENING

Richard Bird

SHOOTING STAR PRESS

A QUANTUM BOOK

Published by Shooting Star Press, Inc.
230 Fifth Avenue, Suite 1212
New York, NY 10001
USA

ISBN 1-57335-468-6

This book was produced by
Quantum Books Ltd
6 Blundell Street
London N7 9BH

CONTENTS

1 WHY ORGANIC GARDENING?

HAT IS ORGANIC GARDENING? The answer is simple: it is gardening that uses only those materials that occur naturally: no artificial fertilizers or chemical sprays. It involves working with nature rather than against it.

In spite of its current popularity, organic gardening is not a new idea. It is the way in which gardeners have gone about their business for generations. Many rural gardeners in America, Britain, and most other countries still do not use any chemicals and would wonder what the fuss was about. Fortunately, this reservoir of knowledge has not been lost and forms the basis of today's organic gardening.

Unfortunately, the media has given the impression that organic gardening is part and parcel of an "alternative" lifestyle. While "new agers" may champion organic growing, it can fit in perfectly happily with any lifestyle and is still relevant to modern living in the same way that legs still are for getting around in the age of the automobile.

RIGHT A well-run organic garden should be an attractive as well as a productive enterprise – both a pleasurable place to work, and a healthy one.

OPPOSITE Organic gardening allows for cultivation of a very wide range of produce, bringing a varied and constant supply of fresh vegetables to the kitchen.

~ WHAT ARE THE ADVANTAGES? ~

There are many reasons why a gardener should think seriously about using organic techniques. The most important, many people would argue, is that man-made chemicals are not used. There are several strands to this argument. First, the earth is slowly becoming polluted with chemicals which do not occur naturally. These are getting into the food chain and have many harmful side-effects. Some are chemicals used to protect crops, such as insecticides and fungicides. Others are used for convenience, for example, the sprays that are applied to prevent apples from dropping off the trees until they are ready to be picked. A larger category of chemicals is used to combat weeds, namely herbicides or weed killers. One of the biggest categories is the artificial fertilizers that are added to the soil to boost production.

BELOW *It is not until gardeners taste their own freshly picked organic fruit and vegetables that they realize the great contrast with the pale imitations sold in most stores today.*

Many of these chemicals are persistent, with side effects lingering long after their original use. DDT is a prime example. Although it has been banned for many years, it still exists in the soil and affects animal and even human populations. The excessive use of artificial fertilizers has led to their runoff into streams and rivers, which has raised the nitrate levels in drinking water. The implications of this are still being assessed.

Although pronounced safe, the long-term side effects of eating vegetables and fruit which contain the residues of sprays and plant feeds is not yet known. When we see the dwindling bird populations, for example, we cannot escape the conclusion that man's additions to the soil and atmosphere have something to do with this and that sooner or later we will be on the receiving end ourselves.

The short-term effects are often apparent. Most people have had stomach complaints after eating too close to the eye of an apple in which spray residues have remained in spite of washing. They often dismiss it as an "upset stomach" without giving any thought as to the cause. Many unexplained headaches and fevers may well be caused by the food we eat. Whether this is so or not, most people eating organically grown produce feel happier and healthier.

There are also the effects on the countryside – our native wild flowers and the insects that feed on them. Reduce the number of flowering plants and the number of butterflies and bees will also drop.

You may feel that the blame for all this can be put on the farmers, but the gardening community utilizes a great deal of land and has just as much responsibility not to pollute and destroy it. What is more, if you grow your own vegetables at least some of what you eat and your subsequent health is in your own hands.

The misuse of chemicals is as much a moral as a practical consideration as it is likely to affect unborn generations as much as our own. However, traditional country dwellers have more immediate and personal reasons for following organic practice. The first is that organically grown food undoubtedly tastes a

ABOVE *Organic gardening involves working with nature. Rather than kill off all insects you should encourage the beneficial ones, such as this hoverfly, which naturally prey on others that harm plants. Pesticides do not pick and choose!*

and is likely to impoverish the soil in the long run. If you can improve on your investment, as well as reaping increased benefits from it, that is surely the road to take.

One of the basic tenets of organic gardening is to diversify: pests and diseases are much more likely to attack a monocrop than a mixed one. It follows that an organic garden is often one of variety, especially in the flower gardens. This produces a colorful scene, especially as organic gardening encourages a wide range of butterflies and bees.

One final word about chemicals. If handled correctly, chemicals should be safe to the user. Unfortunately, all gardeners are human and accidents happen all too frequently. Sprays get into the eyes or are inadvertently swallowed. There are many accidents each year, a large number of them fatal, involving young children and chemicals which have not been locked securely away. No amount of warning labels or legislation is going to prevent carelessness. If there are no chemicals around the risk is eliminated.

Chemicals can often harm plants as well. Inorganic fertilizers that fall onto a plant instead of the ground can "burn" the leaves. Similarly, not all chemical insecticides are suitable for all plants. Some plants which react badly to certain sprays are mentioned on the label, but there are many that are not and if you collect a wide range of ornamental plants you are bound to have some that can be maimed or killed by certain insecticides.

whole lot better. The flavor and texture of tomatoes that have been grown organically are much better than those grown with artificial fertilizers.

It is not only the flavor that has kept many gardeners from using chemicals. There is the cost. Organic material can be created by returning all garden waste to the soil, a cheap process. Inorganics are expensive. The same is true of chemical sprays. If you create a garden in which pests are not a problem, you save a lot on the cost of chemicals (and the cost of their packaging and advertising, which is probably more than that of the chemicals).

Another factor of which traditional gardeners are aware is that by adding organic material to the soil you are constantly improving it. Pouring chemicals into the soil does little other than give an immediate return

---

ADVANTAGES OF ORGANIC GARDENING

- Produces food free from alien chemicals
- Improves the soil
- Produces tastier food
- Produces cheaper food
- Produces a wider range of ornamental plants
- Produces an attractive garden
- Encourages wildlife
- Avoids polluting the environment
- Avoids having dangerous chemicals in the garden

WHAT ARE THE IMPLICATIONS FOR THE ORGANIC GARDENER?

Apart from better food and a better garden, there is not a great deal of difference between organic gardening and that using chemicals. The size and quality of produce is not impaired, and are likely to be improved, especially the taste. The organic gardener is just as capable of exhibiting vegetables and flowers at local fairs and shows.

Not a great deal of extra time is involved and that time is well spent, as gardening is very healthy exercise! Depending on evening light and the weather, an hour a day, with perhaps a little extra at peak times, will enable any gardener to do a tremendous amount. I cope with 1.5 acres of vegetable gardens and ornamental borders working to this kind of schedule. However, the fair-weather gardener who lets the season start ahead of him will have an uphill battle once the weeds have gained the upper hand. Little and often is the key to success. In this way any problems, such as pests or diseases, which crop up can be spotted early on and dealt with before they become serious.

All this, of course, applies to all gardeners. Where the organic gardener is different is that he or she does not keep rushing off to the municipal dump with garden refuse, but

BELOW To all outward appearances the differences between chemical and organic vegetable gardening are not that major. But a closer look at the latter reveals better soil structure and tastier produce.

compositss or shreds it and returns it to the soil. They do not spend hours scrubbing their hands, hoping they have removed all the chemical insecticide that got on them while spraying. They do not count the days before they can eat a cabbage which has been sprayed against caterpillars, nor do they pray for windless days so they can spray weeds without drift getting on to other plants.

The organic gardener will spend time making a compost heap and occasionally turning it. He will spend time adding this to the soil, but not much more than he would if he were frequently dosing it with chemical fertilizers. He will spend time picking caterpillars from a cabbage by hand, but at least

ABOVE A *flower garden is distinctively organic when native species can be seen among the normal border cultivars. These "wild" flowers will both attract beneficial insects and act as a decoy for pests.*

he can eat it right away. He will spend time hoeing, mulching, and hand weeding. He is liable to think more about what he is doing; if a problem occurs he will think of a positive solution rather than reach for a can of chemicals.

In other words, the organic gardener drops a few of the processes that involve chemicals and substitutes other. As much as anything, a change to organic gardening means a change of attitude. Organic gardening is not an easy option, but then no gardening, if carried out properly, is. You get out of it what you put in. Because of his greater involvement in what he is doing, the organic gardener will learn more and be more aware of nature around him. In consequence, he will be a better gardener.

PLANNING THE ORGANIC GARDEN

HETHER YOUR GARDEN IS TO BE organic or not, the first thing to decide is exactly what you want from it. The demands on the space next to a house can be great. Your first priority may be vegetables, or flower borders, or both. However, if you have children they will want somewhere to play, not only with footballs and baseballs but also with bicycles and skateboards.

BELOW *Many equate organic gardening with an offbeat, "alternative" lifestyle, but there is no reason why such a garden should not be as tidy and traditional-looking as others.*

People use their yards and gardens for relaxation and entertaining. A patio or terrace, possibly with a barbecue or even a swimming pool, might well be on the agenda. There are always a few eyesores in a garden – garbage cans, compost heaps, toolsheds – which need space somewhere, preferably out of sight. Then there are the paths and lawns that connect all these together.

All these different demands on the garden space must be taken into account before laboriously preparing a wonderful vegetable patch. If the garden is not very large, you may not be able to do everything you want to. You will have to compromise and grow herbs in the flower beds, for example, or have a separate herb garden and drop all ideas of creating a pond. It may not be necessary to have both a paved patio and a lawn. Some things can be put off until the children are less demanding on play space.

Space is not the only criterion to consider when planning the garden; time is another vital factor. It is no good creating an acre of vegetable garden and an acre of flower beds unless you have the time to attend to them. It is better to start on a smaller scale and gradually add to it as you become aware of your capabilities.

The first step in planning the garden then is to draw up a list of what you want from it, restricting this to what you can achieve within the space and time available.

CHECKLIST OF POSSIBLE GARDEN AREAS

- Vegetable plot
- Flower borders
- Herb garden
- Fruit garden
- Wild garden
- Ornamental ponds/pools
- Lawns
- Patio/terraces
- Paths
- Greenhouses/sheds/garage
- Swimming pool
- Barbecue areas
- Arbors/flowering arches and trellises
- Garbage cans
- Compost containers/leaf mold pens
- Play areas/sandboxes/swings

RIGHT *Plan the layout as you would for any garden, allocating space to all the different activities that are likely to take place. Greenhouse and utility areas should be integrated into the design.*

WHAT GOES WHERE?

Having decided on your priorities, the next task is to allocate the space available within the garden. Some areas are bound to have more sun than others, some may have better soil, some may be damper. Some activities are better done near the house, while it does not matter where others are located. If your first priority is to grow good vegetables, the best position in terms of soil and sun should be given over to these. It is no good choosing a shady or damp area. Vegetables like sun and air. Nowadays, vegetables are usually relegated to the bottom of the yard, but in traditional cottage gardens they often started right outside the back door so that the cook did not have far to go. However, as long as there is a good path from the house to the vegetable garden you can put it anywhere, as long as the site meets the above criteria.

Ornamental borders are a bit more flexible. Although most flowering plants prefer a sunny position, there are many that will tolerate shade. However, flowers are meant to be seen, if possible from the house or from a patio or a lawn where people sit and relax.

Patios are usually constructed near the house, convenient for carrying things in and out. If this is an area in full shade, however, it would probably be better to move it elsewhere.

Utility areas for keeping garbage cans and the like can be tucked away out of sight, but as they are used a great deal they should not be too far from the house. Likewise, compost containers should not be inaccessible because the organic gardener is constantly adding to them. You should add all the garden waste to them, as well as any uncooked vegetable waste – peelings, outer fallen leaves, teabags, and the like.

LEFT When laying out the garden, remember that vegetables are often pretty to look at and can be combined effectively, as here, with flowering plants. Beyond aesthetics, there are often other mutual benefits, particularly in terms of beneficial insects.

Keep all leaves. You can compost them if there are not very many or keep them in a separate leaf mold pen, sited at the same place. In recent years many gardeners have acquired shredders so that even quite large stems of woody material can be composted or used as mulch. Although there are gasoline-engine models, many are powered by electricity, so the area in which a shredder is used should be near a power supply.

There are many similar points, some of which may seem minor, which if taken into consideration when you are first planning the garden will save a lot of time and frustration later on. Spend a lot of time wandering around the garden, looking at it. If weeds are growing better in one part than another this may well be where the soil is best. Dig samples from several places to find out how the soil varies throughout the garden. Notice which parts have sun for the whole day and which parts for only a short while. Perhaps a large tree casts shadow over more of the garden than you realized.

One final ingredient is required: the style. You might want a formal layout with plenty of straight lines and symmetrical beds, or a garden with sinuous curves where the visitor wonders what lies around the corner. Perhaps a cottage garden style is more to your taste, integrating vegetables and flowers in one bed, a subject we shall return to later. You may just want to use up every available square inch of ground. The plants will not care about the aesthetics of the garden, but some gardeners are more conscious of them than others, so it is a factor which you should take into account.

DESIGNING THE GARDEN

With all this information you can begin to lay out the garden. Many people like to sketch it out on paper – not the detailed planting, just rough sketches as to what goes where. Others prefer to do it on the actual ground, using garden hose or string to give the outlines of beds. Another way is to hoe the outlines as a trench in the weeds or scratch them in the bare earth. It does not matter which method

you use as long as you can get an overall impression of what the garden will be like so you can make sure you have everything in the right place.

Once it is drawn out on paper or on the ground, look at it from all angles: from the key windows of the house to see what you will be looking at and from any area outside where you are likely to sit. In both cases you will want to look at flowers rather than compost boxes. Mark out the paths to see how far you will have to walk to put out the garbage, or whether you can snatch a few herbs on a wet day without having to dress for an expedition. Check that any areas you may have set aside for wildlife are away from noise and disturbance, such as a neighbor's dog, and that the flight path of bees from any proposed hives does not take them across public areas or in through the kitchen window.

Once you are satisfied, it is time to start gardening. The first task is to prepare the soil. Once that is done, the detailed planning of the vegetable garden and flower beds can be considered before you start planting. This planning will be dealt with in the relevant chapters.

LEFT *Beds need not be on a large scale. Here, they are broken down into small plots so that the gardener can move freely among the herbs and other plants. This is not only visually attractive but a very practical solution.*

3 LOOKING AFTER THE SOIL

THE SOIL IS THE MOST important part of your garden; from it all goodness flows. If you ignore your soil and continue to sow and plant each year without returning anything to it, the productivity and quality of the vegetables and other plants will diminish noticeably. To produce of its best it must be treated as a friend; it needs to be fed and watered, and not compacted by being trodden on when it is too wet.

If you can achieve a fertile soil, one which is moisture retentive yet free draining, the chances of producing good vegetables and flowers will be much greater. The vegetables will have more weight and flavor while the flowering plants will increase in vigor and produce more flowers. At the same time both will stand up better to pests and diseases. Poor soil will produce weak, sickly plants which will not be much credit to you as a gardener and will also be prone to all kinds of problems.

SOIL STRUCTURE

Soils are basically broken down rock. As such, they are inert and not much use for supporting plant life. However, incorporated into this is a lot of organic material which not only provides nutrients but also the fibrous material that is essential for the soil's moisture-holding capacity. Without it, water would drain away very quickly, as through sand. There are other ways in which nutrients find their way into the soil, by washing down from the mountains, for example, but for our purposes we can assume that most naturally occurring food for our plants comes from organic materials.

The composition of the soil can vary dramatically, depending on how it was formed. Sandy soils are very light, free draining, and friable (crumbly). They do not hold moisture well and this passage of water also carries (leaches) nutrients away with it.

Clay soils are made up of fine particles which stick together, giving the tackiness charactertistic of clay. Clay is very slow draining so that soils composed of it create a wet, sticky environment in which few plants are happy. The clammy soil is also very difficult to work. Once clay soils dry out they become as hard as

IDENTIFYING SOIL LAYERS

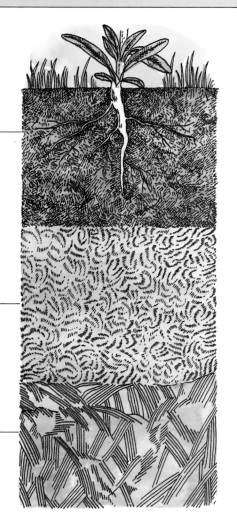

Topsoil The darkest and richest part of the profile and usually a spade's depth, this is chiefly where plants grow. This is also where most of the worms, bacteria, and insects are found, many of them beneficial to plant growth.

Subsoil This is not as fertile as the topsoil but the gardener should try to improve it by double digging (see page 29) and adding organic material.

Parent matter This layer consists mainly of unaltered rock, and is well beyond the reach of most plants.

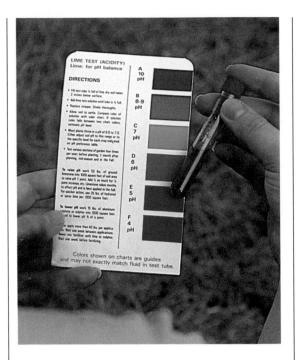

RIGHT *Although it is possible to tell roughly what type of soil is in the garden by looking at the surrounding vegetation, it is much better to make a complete soil analysis with a pH test kit, taking samples from various parts of the garden.*

iron, producing a hostile environment for most garden plants. Again, dry clay is very difficult to work.

In between these two soils there is the happy medium known as loam. This is moisture retentive, so there is enough water for the plants, but at the same time free draining so that any excess water drains away. Good loam is a joy to work. Both sandy and clay soils can be improved to form good, fertile loam.

Depending on the base rock or main component, a soil can be either acid or alkaline. Soils associated with peaty areas are acid, while others that lie over chalk or limestone are alkaline. Very few plants will tolerate the extremes of either. Some, calcifuges, will not grow on alkaline soils, rhododendrons being a classic example. Others, calcioles, will not grow in acid conditions, dianthus, for example.

The relative acidity/alkalinity of soils is measured on a pH scale from 0 to 14, of which 7 is neutral. The best soil from a gardener's point of view is just on the acid side of neutral, at about 6.5. Most vegetables will grow at about 6 to 6.8, a lot tolerating a wider range from about 5 to 8, although this is not ideal. Below this the soil is too acid and will lock up a lot of the minerals that plants need. Above it soils become too alkaline, which will have a similar effect. Fortunately, both sandy/clay soils and

acid/alkaline soils can be modified to meet our needs.

However, before looking into methods of achieving this, one more aspect of soil structure must be considered: the soil profile. Generally in a garden the top spade depth comprises the best soil. This is known as the topsoil. This topsoil has usually been worked as either garden or agricultural soil for centuries and has changed from the underlying soil. The layer beneath the topsoil is known as the subsoil. In many situations this is the native soil, but in well-worked gardens this has also been worked on and improved to at least another spade depth. Below this is the true subsoil, which in a clay area, for example, is likely to be pure clay. It is essential that the gardener keeps these layers in their respective places. To bring subsoil to the surface and bury the topsoil is to lose years of accumulated goodness.

Another factor is where a "hardpan" is produced between the different layers of soil. Years of constant plowing or digging can form a compacted layer at the depth of the plow or spade, through which neither water, air, nor roots can pass. Chemicals, particularly minerals, leached through the soil tend to build up on this pan, often making it all the harder and possibly toxic to plants. This is only a problem if it is not spotted, as it can be broken up by deep digging.

SOIL ANALYSIS

It should be obvious by digging a hole in the garden and then running some of the soil through your fingers whether you have a sandy or clay soil. If you put a sample in a glass jar with some water and then shake it up, you will see the different components settle down into layers, with any organic material floating at the top.

To check on its ability to retain or lose water, dig a hole of one spade depth and fill it with water. Let it drain away and then fill the hole again. If this second filling disappears rapidly, the soil is far too free draining. On the other hand, if it is still there after several hours, or worse still several days, it is nowhere near free draining enough. If it disappears at a steady rate over half an hour or so then the balance is about right.

There are several natural indicators as to the acidity or alkalinity of your soil. If bracken (*Pteridium aquilinum*) or rhododendrons grow in the garden then it is on the acid side. Better still, however, is to get a soil-testing kit from a garden center. Some are basic kits which will simply tell you the pH (the relative acidity/alkalinity of soil), while others will test for the presence and concentration of the naturally occurring chemicals that plants need for growth. Most are simple to operate by following the instructions on the package. Be sure to take several tests, sampling the soil from different parts of each plot to get an average reading.

~

IMPROVING THE SOIL

~

Once you have analyzed your soil it is possible to see what can be done to improve it. Light soils such as the sandy ones should be beefed up by adding well-rotted organic material to them. This will help hold the moisture and at the same time provide a lot of the nutrition plants need. At first, the ground seems to gobble up the compost whatever it may be and it rapidly disappears, but over the months and years the soil will gradually improve until it is much more moisture retentive.

Clay soils are more problematic to deal with, particularly as they are heavy and difficult to work. Sharp sand and small stones in the form of gravel help a great deal. Although one does not normally think of gardening on stone, there is no doubt that adding these materials greatly improves the drainage. They will also break up the soil and make it easier to work. If you burn pestilent weeds the bonfire ash will usually contain fired particles of earth which were clinging to the roots. The heat of the fire will have dried these to an almost potterylike hardness and they will not return again to being soil, making them, like grit, an ideal addition to a clay soil to help break it up.

Organic material in the form of compost or farmyard manure will also help to transform the soil into a lighter medium. Worms constantly break it down and mix it into the soil. Another advantage of compost and other forms of organic material is that they darken the soil, which helps to warm it up more quickly after winter. There are many more reasons for using organic material and we come to these later in this chapter.

An alternative to both soils is to create a raised bed using boards and fill this with a mixture of compost and brought-in loam, effectively turning the topsoil into the subsoil. Eventually the worms will work a lot of this top layer down so that the original topsoil becomes fertile and useable, but there is no reason why you cannot use the raised beds indefinitely.

The best average pH for most garden plants is 6.5. For soils which have a lower value than this (acidic soils) lime in one of its forms can be added until the pH reaches this figure. You can buy lime either as ground limestone (or ground chalk), quicklime (unslaked lime), slaked lime, or magnesium limestone at all garden centers.

COMPOSITION OF ORGANIC MATERIALS			
Material	% Nitrogen	% Phosphorus	% Potassium
Blood meal	15	1.3	0.7
Bone meal	4	22	0.2
Bracken	2	0.2	0.5
Cow manure (fresh)	3	0.2	0.4
Cow manure (old)	0.6	0.4	0.4
Dried blood	12–14	2.5	0.5
Fish meal	10	3.0	0
Guano	12	8.0	3.0
Hoof and horn	13	1.5	0
Horse manure (fresh)	0.4	0.2	0.4
Horse manure (old)	0.7	0.5	0.6
Leaf mold	0.5	0.2	0.3
Pig manure	0.6	0.5	0.3
Poultry manure	2	1.8	1.4
Rock phosphate	0	20	0
Rock potash	0	0	11
Seaweed	1	0.5	4
Sheep manure	0.7	0.4	0.3
Straw	0.6	0.3	0.9
Used hops	1	0.8	0.3
Used mushroom compost	0.6	0.3	0.8

These are naturally occurring substances so do no harm to the soil or to the plants, as long as you do not use them to excess. The quantities to apply to different soils are usually given on the packaging. They can be scattered on to freshly turned soil and left to weather in before replanting. If plants are already in the ground, avoid contact with the lime.

Unfortunately, it is not as easy to do the reverse process, namely, reduce a high pH (alkaline soils) value to 6.5. You can achieve this in small areas by adding acid materials, such as peat (but see page 24) or acidic leaf molds, but the chalk soon leaches back in. If you want to grow lime-hating plants in chalky areas it is best to grow them in tubs of specially imported soil, away from contact with your native soil.

DRAINAGE

Drainage is an important part of soil improvement. It is no good trying to grow anything other than wet-loving plants in areas which are waterlogged. It may be a relatively simple matter of adding sharp sand or gravel as mentioned above, but if it is a serious problem, with water lying on the ground after every shower of rain, you must install a proper drainage system. This is done by digging trenches, in a herringbone pattern, down into the subsoil and laying drainage pipes in them. Cover them with small stones or simply fill the trenches with rocks and rubble topped with gravel. Water should be led away to a drainage ditch if there is one, or into a soakaway. This is a deep hole of at least a cubic yard's capacity which is filled with rubble. An alternative, if the lie of the land permits, is to make use of the water by creating a pond and leading the pipes into it.

COMPOST

Compost is one of the organic gardener's most important means of achieving a productive soil. Every year in the wild nature returns much of the goodness that has gone into creating plants back to the soil: trees drop their leaves (even evergreens drop leaves, but not all at once) and herbaceous plants die back. This cycle is a continuous one, but if you break it, as one does in the garden, by removing the vegetables to eat, you have to find some other way to add organic material to the soil.

The non-organic gardener uses artificial fertilizers. While these feed the plants, they do not condition the soil in other ways. A much more sensible and natural way is to recycle all the organic matter one can – weeds, grass cuttings, vegetable waste, and leaves – and return it to the soil. If available in sufficient quantities this should be enough to keep most gardens going, just occasionally supplemented with naturally occurring, organic fertilizers to replace specific minerals which may be in short supply.

There are various ways of composting waste. You can buy special boxes for the purpose which come in a variety of designs. You can also make your own boxes from brick or timber. It is the practice in country areas simply to stack all the composting materials in a heap. This might not be the most efficient method but it is certainly the cheapest.

There are three basic requirements for a good compost heap. The heap needs to retain

RIGHT *Some valuable materials for improving soil quality;* **1** *Bone meal;* **2** *manure;* **3** *grass cuttings;* **4** *peat;* **5** *used bark;* **6** *rock potash.*

POSSIBLE COMPOST INGREDIENTS	
From the garden	**From the kitchen**
• Weeds • Plant debris • Leaves • Non-woody stalks • Shredded woody material • Animal manure (not cat or dog) • Grass clippings • Straw (small quantities) • Wood shavings (small quantities) • Activator (see text) • Sprinkling of lime	• Uncooked vegetable waste • Uncooked fruit waste • Old cut flowers • Tea leaves and teabags • Coffee grounds • Crushed eggshells
COMPOST INGREDIENTS TO AVOID	
• Diseased plant material • Pernicious weeds • Weeds or plants containing seed • Cooked or animal kitchen waste • Dog or cat manure • Woody material that has not been crushed or shredded	

the heat it generates, sufficient air, and enough moisture without being over wet. These requirements can be met by constructing a box which has sides and a lid to keep in the heat and keep out excessive moisture, and holes in it to allow air to enter. Quite a number of commercial and homemade designs are available.

Any scrap vegetative material can be used, even kitchen waste as long as it has not been cooked (this may attract rats and other vermin). There are a few things to avoid. For example, do not add diseased plants to the heap, otherwise you are likely to perpetuate the problem. Similarly, be cautious about adding pernicious perennial weeds and weeds which are in seed. In theory, the temperature of the compost should destroy both, but there are usually a lot left, especially around the edges of the heap, which may not heat up.

There are ways around this. Leave persistent weeds, such as quack grass (*Agropyron repens*), lying out in the sun until they are dead. Put weeds and other plants in seed into a separate heap or box and only use them for deep planting, around the roots of a tree or shrub, for example. Any seed will be deep out of harm's way and unlikely to be disturbed and brought to the surface where it will germinate. Crush tough material like cabbage stalks and thick flower stems before adding them to the heap. Alternatively, they can be shredded (see page 24).

Put the materials into the box or heap, making sure that they are either in shallow layers or thoroughly mixed. Avoid creating thick layers, especially of materials such as grass clippings which will mat down into a thick, slimy, and impenetrable mass. If the materials are all mixed up, air can circulate

COMPOST CONTAINERS

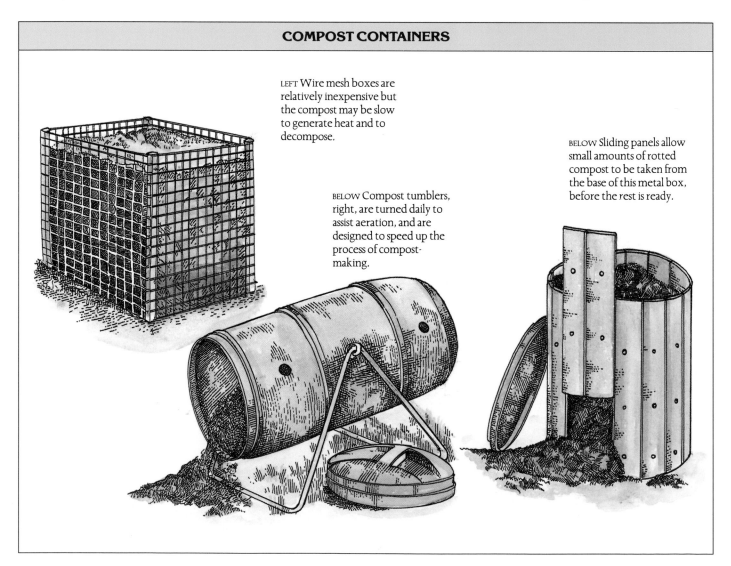

LEFT Wire mesh boxes are relatively inexpensive but the compost may be slow to generate heat and to decompose.

BELOW Compost tumblers, right, are turned daily to assist aeration, and are designed to speed up the process of compost-making.

BELOW Sliding panels allow small amounts of rotted compost to be taken from the base of this metal box, before the rest is ready.

BUILDING YOUR OWN COMPOST BOX

Homemade boxes are usually cheaper and can be made to measure. It is a good idea to have three boxes side by side, as illustrated, so that the first can be used for fresh waste, the second for part-rotted waste, while using well-rotted compost from the third.

freely, nourishing the bacteria that are getting on with the job of breaking everything down. Although it does not seem to be such common practice today, many gardeners put down brushwood as the first layer, to help the air to circulate through the compost.

Bacteria also need nitrogen. Some will be obtained from the contents of the heap but you want to put as much nitrogen as you can into the soil, so it is a good idea to supplement this. A little farmyard manure is a great benefit. If this is not available you can buy organic activators from most garden centers. The process can be a bit acid and it helps to add a light sprinkling of ground limestone every foot (30 cm) or so as the heap builds up.

The heap should be moist but not soaked. Once it is wet enough to put a lid on it (a sheet of polyethylene will do), both to keep excess rain out and to keep heat in. Turning will help to aerate the heap and also to bring in to the middle material from the outside of the heap, where it breaks down more slowly. Some commercial compost boxes consist of a barrel which can be rotated on a stand, making it

very easy to mix the ingredients without cooling them down as inevitably happens if you do it with a fork.

If the material is simply thrown into a heap, too much heat escapes and, in wet areas, too much water can enter, which apart from anything else helps to cool it down. However, I generate a lot of compost from my large garden and would need innumerable boxes to keep up with it all. So I stack all the compost, the top layer acting as a thatch to shed excess rain. Because I have so much I tend not to hurry about using it. I will often leave one stack from one year to the next spring, when I turn it, bring all the unrotted material on the outside to the middle, and then use it to plant summer squash on. That autumn I use it on the garden. With boxes it is possible to shorten the cycle between adding material and its re-use, often to as little as ten weeks.

Well-rotted compost which is ready for use is friable (crumbly) and not smelly. With more than one box you can be filling one while another is breaking down and you are using up a third.

~ OTHER ORGANIC MATERIALS ~

Many other types of organic material can be added to the soil. They vary in their nutritional value, but all help to condition the soil.

BELOW *Shredded bark is a very useful material in the garden. Its main function is as a mulch, which is spread over borders, creating a warm blanket that holds in moisture and prevents the germination of weeds.*

PEAT

This has become an emotive subject of late as over-zealous extraction has led to the spoliation of many natural habitats. To reduce the damage, many gardeners have given up using peat. In fact, this is quite a wise move as peat is not particularly useful material anyway. It breaks down very quickly in the soil, so is of little use as a conditioner, and it has virtually no nutritional value. Its prime use to the gardener is as a moisture-retentive medium in potting compost. Leaf mold has always been the traditional alternative and now there are many more, including coir or coconut fibers.

SHREDDED MATERIALS

Few modern gadgets are likely to impress the organic gardener as much as the shredder: a machine driven by electricity or gasoline which chops up all the harder garden waste that one would previously have burnt. Depending on the size of the machine it will cope with woody material up to almost branch size. As well as twigs, prunings, and hedge clippings, shredders also cope with the woodier flower stalks and tough cabbage stalks. The resulting material should be stacked for at least six months and then it can be used as a mulch. This is an invaluable way of returning waste material to the garden.

SHREDDED OR CHIPPED BARK

The potential use of bark as a by-product of the timber trade has finally been realized and it is now becoming increasingly available to gardeners. It mainly comes from conifers and should be stacked for a few months to allow any resin fumes, which may otherwise harm plants, to evaporate. It is not particularly nutritious, but when well rotted can make a good addition to the soil because of its moisture-retentive properties. As a mulch it is excellent. It takes quite a while to break down and therefore lasts a long time on the surface. It does require nitrogen for decomposition and will remove this from the soil, so it is essential to top-dress the soil beneath with a nitrogen-rich fertilizer of some sort, well-rotted farmyard manure, or an organic fertilizer such as seaweed meal or dried blood.

LEAF MOLD

One of nature's additions to the soil is leaves, both those of deciduous trees that fall in autumn and those of evergreens that fall throughout the year. Leaf mold is an invaluable material for gardeners and leaves should never be burnt, no matter how nice an autumn bonfire may smell. Make a wire cage and pile all the leaves that you can find into it. However, *never* take them from woods as the trees depend on leaf mold for their continuing existence. Leaves take a long time to break down, but, once they have, a huge heap is reduced to a small one, so you need to collect as many as possible. Once broken down, leaf mold is a dark, crumbly material which is excellent for mulching, adding to the soil, or for mixing into potting composts as an alternative to peat.

FARMYARD MANURE

Traditionally, this is one of the best soil conditioners. It contains plenty of fibrous material and plenty of nutrients. Farmyard manure consists of dung and usually the bedding material of various animals – cows, horses, pigs, chicken, goats, and sheep. All are good but many gardeners prefer them in the order given, with cow manure being the best. However, opinions vary just as much as to which is the best beer.

All farmyard manure should be well rotted. You can tell when it is ready to use as it crumbles in the hand and is odourless. Some that have a high urea content, such as poultry manure, will damage the plants unless they have been stacked until this has evaporated or broken down; again, lack of smell is a good indicator. Once ready, usually after about six months, poultry fertilizer can be very potent and should be used sparingly. It makes a good activator for compost heaps.

Farmyard manure which includes straw bedding, such as horse manure, may also contain insecticide and herbicide residues. If there is any doubt about this have a sample analyzed before you use it. What it is certain to contain is weed seed. Manure is good for digging deep into the soil but it can produce a rash of seedlings if it is used as a top-dressing.

ABOVE A *crude but effective compost box, the lid of which helps to keep out excessive rain. This is important since waterlogging of organic material slows down or even stops the rotting process, as well as leaching out valuable nutrients.*

Many stables now use wood shavings as bedding and this is more likely to be sterile.

Farmyard manure became difficult to find with the rise of battery farming. Try to find a farmer who grazes animals outside, or a riding school or stables. In fact, many stables have a big problem with disposal. They are more than grateful to anyone who can take some off their hands and it can be had for the carrying away.

USED MUSHROOM COMPOST

Mushroom farms have to keep renewing the material on which they grow mushrooms and have the problem of disposing of the old material. It is usually chopped bracken laced with horse manure, an ideal combination for the garden. Most also have a small amount of lime added. This is generally to the benefit of the garden but if you want to grow ericaceous plants, such as heather or rhododendrons, it is best avoided, at least in areas of the garden where these are to grow. Used mushroom compost can be used as a soil conditioner or as a mulch.

SEAWEED

Gardeners who live near the coast have long considered seaweed one of the best materials to add to the soil. It is particularly rich in minerals. Seaweed also contains growth hormones which help to promote healthy plants. Seaweed rots down quite quickly and many gardeners and farmers use it directly on the soil, but it can be stacked like all other manures. Gardeners inland can buy dried seaweed. It can be used as a soil additive, a top-dressing as a fertilizer, or as an activator in compost heaps.

OTHER ORGANIC MATERIALS

There is a wide range of organic materials which can be used in the garden. Many of these are waste products of industrial processes. Used hops, for example, are distillery by-products, and gardeners have applied them as soil conditioners and mulches for years. Similarly, husks of the cocoa bean have become popular. Do not use material which may have come into contact with non-organic chemicals.

GREEN MANURES

One normally thinks of composts and manures as being waste products which are usually dead. But one very good form of compost is very much alive, at least until it is dug into the soil. This is green manure. The advantage of conventional compost is that it is produced away from the beds and can be used when it is required. Green manure only works if you have the space and time between crops to grow it.

The idea is to plant a quick growing crop which will add valuable nutrients and organic material to the soil when it is dug in. Some, such as the pea family, clovers, or lupines for example, are very good at "fixing" or holding nitrogen into the soil. Others, buckwheat for example, are used just because they are a quick way of introducing nutrient-rich material into the soil. As well as providing nutrients, green manures can help prevent soil erosion in exposed areas while there is no other crop in the ground. Plants should be dug into the ground before they flower; the best time is just as the first flower buds are forming. If a crop is densely planted, cut it before digging in. Dig it well into the soil.

GREEN MANURES

Nitrogen fixers
- Alfalfa/lucerne (*Medicago sativa*)
- Alsike clover (*Trifolium hybridum*)
- Black medic (*Medicago lupulina*)
- Cowpea (*Vigna unguiculata*)
- Fava beans (broad beans) (*Vicia faba*)
- Lupines (*Lupinus angustifolius*)
- Red clover (*Trifolium pratense*)
- Winter tare (vetch) (*Vicia villosa*)

Non-nitrogen fixers
- Annual ryegrass (*Lolium multiflorum*)
- Buckwheat (*Fagopyrum esculentum*)
- Comfrey (*Symphytum x uplandicum*)
- Millet (*Millium effusum*)
- Mustard (*Sinapis alba*)
- Rye (*Secale cereale*)

ORGANIC FERTILIZERS

Although there are some organic gardeners who do not like to use any fertilizers at all, most are more than happy to use those that are naturally occurring or are made from naturally occurring substances. These are generally applied for their nitrogen, phosphorus, or potassium content. Nitrogen helps to promote the growth of the green parts of the plant, phosphorus is good for the ripening of fruit, while potassium plays a large part in the promotion of flowering and fruiting. Many other trace elements have effects on the plant. Iron, for example, helps with the formation of chlorophyl, as does manganese.

A wide range of safe fertilizers can be used (see table), each serving a different function. Thus blood meal is high in nitrogen and is useful for a quick-growing leaf crop such as spinach. Bone meal, on the other hand, is high in phosphorus and is therefore useful as a general fertilizer to promote flowering and fruiting, an activity required in most ornamental plants, vegetables, and fruit. Some,

particularly the nitrogen-rich fertilizers, quickly leach out of the soil while others are retained and release their goodness only slowly.

Most fertilizers should be applied when the soil is prepared. Later in the season it can be applied to the surface of the soil, but it must be hoed and then watered in.

LIQUID FERTILIZERS

Once the plants are growing, it is useful to apply any supplementary fertilizer as a liquid feed. These can easily be made by putting some compost or manure into a burlap sack and soaking this in a bucket of water for a couple of weeks, occasionally agitating it. For larger quantities, you can use a barrel. Water the resulting liquid onto the ground around the plants. This is particularly useful where planting is intense. A foliar feed, where the plant absorbs the fertilizer through the leaves, can be made from seaweed extract.

Liquid feeds are only used as supplements. They are no substitute for good soil preparation and enrichment.

OPPOSITE *If time between crops allows, using "green manures" – plants whose long roots draw up nutrients deep down in the soil – are a good way to refresh the earth. They also protect the soil from wind erosion, for example, when no other crops are being grown.*

BELOW *There are several organic fertilizers that can be used to supplement the soil, such as (from left to right) wood ash, compost, blood meal, and bone meal. Unlike inorganic fertilizers these natural products will harm neither the soil nor the vegetables.*

SINGLE DIGGING

For most purposes single digging is sufficient. A trench is dug across the plot and the next spadeful is turned into this, creating a new trench and so down the plot, while organic material is put into the bottom of each trench. The final trench is filled with the soil from the first trench.

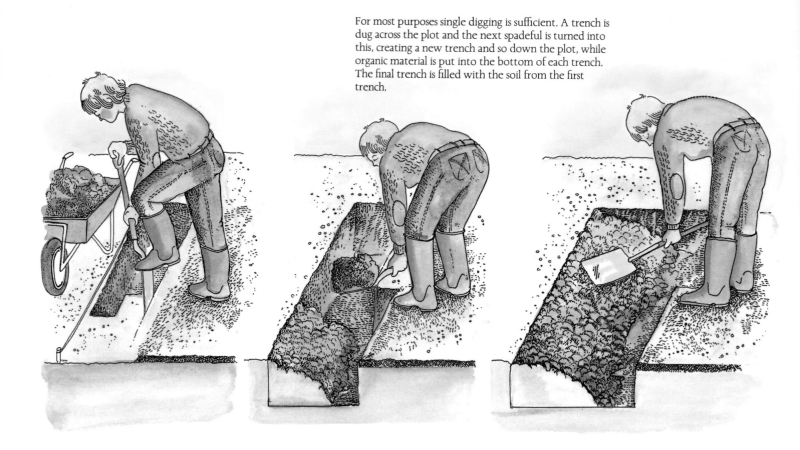

SOIL PREPARATION

In spite of the occasional popularity of "non-dig" methods of cultivation, most gardeners still prefer to dig their plots. The advantages of digging are that it incorporates compost and manures deep into the soil, helps to maintain good drainage, and allows the gardener to see what is happening below the surface, giving him the chance to remove any soil-borne pests, such as wireworms, and deep-rooted weeds.

Once a plot is under cultivation, single digging is all that is required: putting well-rotted compost into the bottom of the trench and turning the next spadeful onto it. However, for the first dig, and every few years thereafter, it is a good idea to double dig the plot so that the bottom layer is broken up, preventing hardpanning and improving its quality.

Digging by hand is preferable to using a machine as you can pause after every spadeful to remove any weeds or pests. A rotary tiller is likely to chop up any weed and spread it far and wide, creating an even worse problem. Remove any perennial weeds as you go and destroy them. Annual weeds can either be removed and composted or they can be dug in, if they are not in seed, well below the surface. If the weeds are tall, cut their tops off before-hand and deal with their roots while you are digging the soil. (For weed control see page 33.)

Once the soil has been dug rotary tillers can be useful in its subsequent breakdown, but they can bring back to the surface all the compost you have laboriously placed at the bottom of the trench. They are useful where the ground to be broken up is heavy and very

DOUBLE DIGGING

Every few years it is a good idea to double dig, to break up any hardpan and enrich the subsoil.

1 Dig a trench, put the soil to one side, and break up the soil in the bottom, adding organic material to it.
2 Dig a new trench, turning the soil from it onto the broken soil in the first trench. Break up the soil in the second trench and continue until the end of the plot is reached. Fill the final trench with the spare soil from the first.

hard work with a hoe and rake. For soil which has been well conditioned and is easy to work these two hand implements take a lot of beating.

As you dig add organic material plus any fertilizers required to redress the balance of the soil. If possible, dig during late autumn, leaving the ground rough to break down under the winter frosts and rain. Never work on the soil when it is wet as this will destroy its structure, compacting it and making it difficult to work.

~

SOIL MAINTENANCE

~

Once the soil has been dug and broken down into a fine tilth it is ready for planting. Do not walk on the soil in wet weather. When planting, it is often better to work from a

plank of wood so that the soil is not compacted. Alternatively, use narrow beds so that you can reach them all from the path. Regular hoeing and hand weeding will keep the weeds down. It is best to follow the maxim, "little and often" rather than let the problem build up and then attempt a blitz on it. An alternative to this is to mulch the soil (see page 34).

For crops which are rarely moved, such as rhubarb, fruit bushes, or herbaceous borders, you can add top-dressings of compost in autumn or spring to replenish the organic material in the soil. If the plants are deep rooted, lightly fork the compost into the soil; otherwise you can leave it to the worms to work it in.

STAYING IN CONTROL

HERE IS A LOT MORE TO gardening than sowing seed and then sitting back to await the harvest. In between these two events weeds will try to colonize the bare soil and pests to gorge themselves on the succulent new growth. It is up to the gardener to prevent both these things happening, so that his own plants not only have the chance to survive but also to grow fat.

The very thought of weeding and pest control is enough to put many people off gardening. But if you undertake these regularly they will cease to be chores. In fact, because of the close contact that you will develop with your plants during these operations, you will learn a great deal.

Many gardeners find that as long as they are on top of the situation, hoeing and weeding can be very relaxing occupations. However, the moment you lose control they become a battle that few enjoy. The secret is "little and often." If weather permits (and evening light if you are away from home during the day), try and put in an hour every day. It is surprising how much you can do in this time.

Another obstacle which nature tends to put in the gardener's path is occasional bad weather. To a large extent the gardener has to learn to live with this, but you can take certain steps to minimize its effect.

COPING WITH THE WEATHER

Gardeners would love to have gentle rain at night and warm sunny days, but things rarely work out like that. Wind, cold weather, and excessive rain are the three things that are sent to torment us.

WIND

This poses several problems. First, wind can simply batter everything to the ground. More subtly, it can dry out both the plants and the ground in summer and sear plants with its icy blast in winter. If the garden is on the coast the wind can also be salt laden, which does not do the plants much good.

Fortunately, wind is one condition that, to a certain extent, the gardener can control. The establishment of windbreaks is a feature of setting up any garden. These may not be essential if you live in an urban environment where buildings and surrounding gardens break

BELOW *An extreme example of wind damage. It is difficult to protect trees of this height, but smaller plants can easily be shielded from stormy weather by creating windbreaks around the garden.*

AVOIDANCE OF FROST POCKETS

1 Frosts often build up at the bottom of a slope, perhaps against a hedge or close fence.
2 This can be avoided by creating a hole to allow the cold air to filter through.
3 A curved, or V-shaped, hedge uphill will also divert the cold air around the frost hollow.

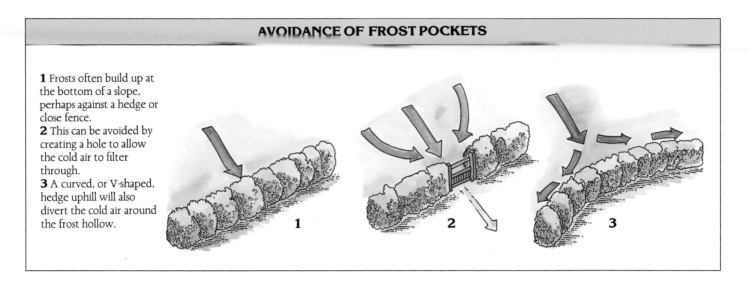

CONTROLLING WIND

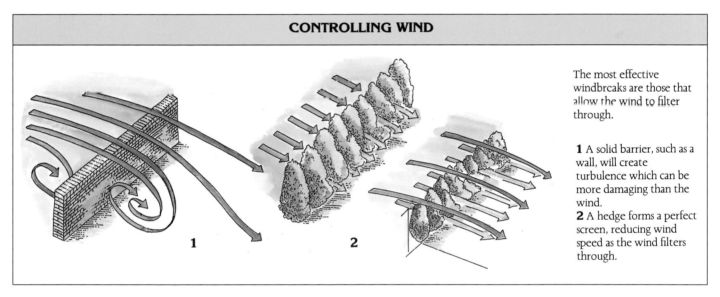

The most effective windbreaks are those that allow the wind to filter through.

1 A solid barrier, such as a wall, will create turbulence which can be more damaging than the wind.
2 A hedge forms a perfect screen, reducing wind speed as the wind filters through.

up the wind, but in rural and other exposed areas they can be vital.

The best form of windbreak is one that allows the wind to filter through. Although a wall or a fence will look solid and appear to be the best defence against strong winds, it actually causes a great deal of turbulence, which can be as devastating as the wind itself. A hedge or row of trees allows the wind to filter through, slowing it down but preventing the great swirl of turbulence that inevitably comes over a wall. Hedges can be either of deciduous or evergreen shrubs or trees. However, if they are deciduous, they must have a thick network of branches to break up the wind during the winter.

Hedges take a while to get established. Those that mature the quickest will, of course, go on growing rapidly and need a lot of

attention to keep neat. Those that are slower to mature will only need to be cut once a year, twice at the most.

Hedges are often considered the poor relations of the garden and, apart from the occasional trim, little is done to them. But to keep hedges at their best they must receive as much attention as any other plants. Double dig the strip where the hedge is to be planted and work in a quantity of organic material. When the hedge has been planted, water it in and mulch it well to help retain moisture and prevent weeds from growing. If the site is windy the hedge itself will need protecting until it has become established. A plastic windbreak is the answer.

Keep the bottom of a hedge weeded and clear of refuse. This will help to promote good health and allow the bottom branches to

ABOVE *Cold weather can be a nuisance in that it can kill unprotected tender plants, but it can be a good thing, too. Among its most valuable assets are that it breaks down the autumn-dug soil into a fine tilth, as well as exposing and killing many harmful insects. It can also be beautiful.*

develop. There is no point in having a hedge under which the wind and animals can creep. Clip the hedge regularly to keep it neat and thick. If it is allowed to get out of control it can become open and sprawling, losing its usefulness as well as encroaching on the garden.

A hedge is not the only form of windbreak available. A much quicker solution is to erect a fence of some sort which will allow the wind to filter through. This can be constructed out of wooden slats or bamboo canes. A modern alternative is to use plastic mesh, which is sold specially for the task. It comes in different grades depending on the percentage of wind it keeps out. This type of windbreak should be firmly anchored and will need renewing every few years.

Another aspect of mastering wind concerns providing the correct support for plants that are liable to blow over. This mainly affects herbaceous plants, but also includes trees and shrubs early in their growth. These will be dealt with in later chapters.

COLD

During the winter cold is no bad thing. It helps to break down the soil and kill off pests which have been brought to the surface layer by digging. But once spring is under way and planting has begun frosts can be a nuisance.

The temperature range across a garden can vary considerably, especially if one part is lower than another. In these lower areas cold air accumulates, forming frost pockets. If the garden is on a slope you can sometimes disperse these or deflect the cold air to prevent them from forming. If the cold air is stopped by a fence or hedge, remove a section or cut a hole in the base to allow the cold air to continue its way down the hill. Any gap can be covered with wire mesh. Alternatively, position a fence or hedge at an angle across the slope above the frost hollow, so that the cold air is deflected to one side and moved off elsewhere.

It is often possible to site some plants which are marginally tender against south-facing walls, which store and reflect heat, making a border in front of them warmer than other parts of the garden. Some vegetables and flowering plants need to be lifted and stored in a frost-free place, while others will take a remarkable degree of frost before they succumb. Some can be left in the soil but will need a mulch of some sort to protect them. These will all be dealt with in later chapters.

RAIN

This can affect the organic garden in three ways. First, there can be too much of it. If this is a permanent weather condition, an effective drainage system must be installed and the soil made free draining. Second, there can be too little. In this case you need to install some form of watering system. You should also add fibrous organic material to the soil, as well as apply a mulch, both aimed at retaining as much moisture in the soil as possible. Types of mulches will be dealt with under weed control.

The third problem is an increasingly desperate one which those affected can do little about. This is the growing incidence of acid rain. While you can counteract the action on the soil by adding lime to keep the pH at around 6.5, little can be done about acid rain which falls on the plants. It is likely to be the longer growing ones, such a trees, that suffer most.

COPING WITH WEEDS

Weeds are typically described as plants which are growing in the wrong place. Most gardeners would agree that fireweed or rosebay willow herb (*Chamaenerion angustifolium*) is an extremely attractive plant when growing in the wild, but few would give it room in a garden as it spreads like crazy.

Weeds take up a lot of the nutrients and water that the gardener wants to be available to his vegetables or flowering plants. They harbor diseases which can be transferred to other plants; groundsel (*Senecio vulgaris*) carries rust fungus, for example. Some sting or scratch the gardener as he works. Others are just ugly and make the garden look a mess.

There are really two types of weeds, the annuals and the more pestilent perennials. The former are not too difficult to deal with and as long as they are removed regularly, so that they are not allowed to seed, they should become a dwindling problem. You can remove them by hoeing or by hand. Hoeing is best done in dry weather when the weeds will shrivel up; if it is wet they may re-root. If they are not diseased or are not seeding you can add them to the compost heap. Burn diseased plants and keep seeding ones in a separate compost heap for use deep down.

Perennial weeds are more of a problem, especially as most increase by spreading underground. To eradicate them all this underground stem must either be removed or prevented from reaching the light, or they will only reshoot. It is usually possible to riddle through a light soil, removing every single piece of the weed. If any remains, pull it out as soon as a shoot appears above the ground. In this way you can clear out most weeds.

On heavy, sticky soil it is a different matter, as odd pieces often remain hidden in a solid lump of soil. One way to cope with this is patiently to keep going through the soil every time a shoot appears. This war of attrition will eventually starve the weed as it will have spent all its available energy trying to get a shoot to the surface. Without light and photosynthesis it cannot produce more food for itself. Another way is to cover the site with a large sheet of black polyethylene or an old rug. This will prevent the weeds from reaching the light and again they will starve. This will take several months and should only be done while the weeds are in active growth. Doing it during the winter is not of much use as the plants are dormant.

Once the beds or borders have been cleared of weeds, you can keep them at bay by laying a mulch. This is a layer of material which is spread over the soil so that light is prevented from reaching it. The best materials are organic, although you can use materials such as polyethylene. Organic materials consist of grass clippings, shredded or chipped bark, compost, and farmyard manures. Grass clippings are excellent, but they can make a border look a

RIGHT *While mulching is a very effective way of keeping new weeds from germinating, it will not smother any perennial weeds already in the soil. It is therefore essential to remove these before the ground is treated.*

bit dull. You should only apply them to about 2 in. (5 cm) deep or they can heat up and harm the plants. Also, if they are piled any deeper they form a slimy mass. With a smaller layer the worms soon take the grass down into the soil. This is extremely beneficial and it is easy enough to add another layer. If it does become too matted, break up the clippings with a fork.

Bark is an ideal material. It is slow to break down and so retains its mulching properties for a long time. Pile it on about 4 in. (10 cm) deep as it will compact. Bark looks a natural material on borders, especially woodland ones.

Used mushroom compost and used hops make good mulches as both are usually sterile. Compost and farmyard manure can contain weed seed, so only use them if you are certain that they are free of it. Some farmyard manures contain wood shavings or sawdust instead of straw, which makes them reasonably free of weed seeds, but there is always likely to be some seed that was in the hay that the livestock ate.

Black plastic is very effective, but terribly ugly. It can blow away and cause problems elsewhere in the countryside. Holes are cut in it and plants inserted through them. It is difficult for water to penetrate once the plastic is in position, although some forms do allow it to percolate through.

It is no good laying an organic mulch on top of weeds; while it may kill off a few annuals, perennials will generally find their way through. It is essential to clear the ground of weeds before mulching. Check areas covered with mulch regularly and remove any seedlings which have grown immediately. If soil has been brought to the surface, by moles for example, cover this with more mulch or weeds might start growing there. As mulch breaks down it will take up nitrogen from the soil, so it is sensible to give the ground a sprinkling of a nitrogen-rich organic fertilizer or a layer of well-rooted farmyard manure before spreading the mulch, so the soil does not become depleted.

Mulches also help to retain moisture in the soil. However, the soil should already be moist before the mulch is applied, otherwise the mulch may take up so much water that none reaches the topsoil.

Similar to the concept of the mulch is that of ground cover – in effect a living mulch. The idea is to cover the ground so closely with plants that there is no room or light for the weeds.

PESTS

Like weeds, pests also try to take advantage of the favourable environment that the gardener is creating. However, it is possible to make life less tolerable for them without resorting to chemical sprays.

GARDEN PESTS

- **Aphids (greenfly)** Suck sap from plants, usually from young growth. Plants become sticky and deformed. *Encourage natural predators (ladybugs, hoverfly, lacewings, mantises). Squash or remove with the fingers, wash off with strong spray of water.*

- **Birds** Remove fruiting buds, steal fruit. *Net the crops during vulnerable periods.*

- **Carrot root fly** Creates tunnels in carrots. *Plant onions nearby. Sow thinly so thinning is not required.*

- **Caterpillars** Eat holes in leaves, often stripping a plant. *Remove eggs before they develop. Pick off caterpillars by hand.*

- **Cucumber beetles** Eat leaves and flowers, often transmitting viral diseases. *Remove by hand or completely cover the plants with fine cheesecloth.*

- **Cutworms** Chew off the roots of a plant just below ground. *Dig around any affected plant and destroy any found. Ground beetles are natural predators.*

- **Earwigs** Cut holes in ornamental flowers and leaves. *Trap in inverted flowerpots filled with straw.*

- **Flea beetles** Make many tiny holes in leaves, especially on cabbages. *As they jump, passing a piece of board covered in grease above young plants will catch many of them.*

- **Leatherjackets** Eat through roots. *Dig around affected area and remove by hand.*

- **Mice** Eat small bulbs and peas. *Trap, either alive or dead, or get a cat.*

- **Rabbits** Plants chewed to the ground. Teeth marks often show. *Put wire mesh around whole garden or individual beds.*

- **Slugs and snails** Holes in leaves and buds. Sometimes will cut right through stems. *Pick by hand at night. Encourage frogs, toads, and birds which eat them.*

- **Tomato horn worm** Holes in leaves and fruit of tomatoes, eggplants, and peppers. *Remove by hand.*

- **Voles (fieldmice)** Chew through stems. *Trap, either alive or dead, or get a cat.*

- **Wireworms** Eat through roots of plants. *Dig around area of affected plants and remove by hand. Trap using potatoes as bait.*

Aphids

Garden slug

GENERAL PESTS

The first rule is to avoid monocultures. If you only grow one type of plant and a pest strikes, it will go through it like wildfire. On the other hand, if you grow a wide selection of plants, only a few are likely to be attacked at any one time. This means that natural predators in the garden are more likely to be able to contain the outbreak.

Another reason for choosing a wide range of flowering plants is that this will encourage a large number of predators, such as ladybugs, hoverflies, lacewings, and mantises. While these are attracted to the nectar of the flowers, their larvae, and sometimes the adults as well, feed on aphids (greenfly) which are one of the main insect pests. It is always a good idea to have a flower garden fairly near a vegetable plot. In some cases it can even help to mix the two.

The choice of plants can be important. Some strains of both vegetables and flowering plants have been selected because they are more resistant to certain pests. It makes sense to use

INSECT TRAPS

A way of monitoring insect pests is to place a few yellow dishes filled with water in different parts of the garden. The insects are attracted to the dishes and drown in the water. This gives a good indication of what pests are around and in what numbers.

ABOVE *Ladybugs are precious friends of the gardener and should not be destroyed or accidentally sprayed. Their larvae eat an incredible quantity of greenfly.*

these. Many of the cottage garden plants that have come down to us have done so because they are tough and have managed to survive without the use of pesticides. A lot of these traditional flowering plants are still widely available and are the ones to choose in preference to many of the modern hybrids that are more prone to pests and disease.

Always check plants that are brought into the garden to see they do not contain pests. Look at the leaves and inspect the soil around the roots to make sure no soil-borne pests are lurking.

Agricultural research has shown that many sorts of predators overwinter in rough grass around the edges of fields. Where these habitats exist the spread of pests back into the fields in the spring is significantly reduced. This research has been taken further by creating grass banks across open fields, with dramatic results. You can emulate this in the garden by keeping strips of long grass to provide winter and early spring shelter for a wide range of predators. Ground beetles and spiders, for example, dispatch an incredible number of pests and such a habitat is perfect for them.

Certain plants deter certain pests from attacking neighbouring plants. Planting onions next to carrots helps to keep carrot root fly away from the latter. Similarly, French marigolds reduce the numbers of Mexican bean beetles and are also very useful for clearing the ground of various destructive nematodes. Some plants act as decoys so that pests attack them rather than the vegetable. For example, mustard attracts at least some of the cabbage butterflies away from the brassicas, reducing the caterpillar nuisance.

Many of the pests that affect trees live in the soil or leaf litter during the winter. A band of grease placed around the trunk prevents them from crawling back up into the branches in the spring.

The final method of pest control is a mechanical one which may not be to everyone's liking. Use your fingers. Squash greenfly when you see them and pick off caterpillars. If you are averse to killing them, transport them far enough away and put them on a similar host plant.

HOSTS TO BENEFICIAL INSECTS

Many flowering plants attract insects which prey on pests. They will never vanquish the pests completely, but will reduce them to tolerable levels.

- **Amaranth** Ground beetles
- **Anise** Beneficial wasps
- **Celery (flower)** Beneficial wasps
- **Chamomile** Hoverflies, beneficial wasps
- **Chervil** Hoverflies, beneficial wasps
- **Clover** Ground beetles, parasites of woolly aphids
- **Dandelion** Beneficial wasps
- **Fennel** Hoverflies, beneficial wasps
- **Goldenrod** Hoverflies, praying mantis
- **Hyssop** Hoverflies, beneficial wasps
- **Ivy** Hoverflies, beneficial wasps
- **Marigold** Hoverflies
- **Milkweed** Several parasites
- **Mint** Hoverflies, beneficial wasps
- **Mustard** Various parasites
- **Soybean** Benificial wasps
- **Nettle** Many beneficial insects
- **Sunflower** Lacewings, beneficial wasps
- **Tansy** Ladybugs
- **Yarrow** Ladybugs, beneficial wasps

LARGER PESTS

Slugs and snails are among the gardener's worse enemies, but most gardeners prefer not to use chemical bait which can also affect other wildlife. The simplest method is to trap them under a piece of tile or an upturned grapefruit peel and then dispose of them. Another method is to go out at night with a flashlight and gather them by hand. You will be surprised at first at how many there are, but after a few nights' foraying you will have reduced the numbers to an acceptable level. The easiest way of killing slugs is to put them into a jar or water containing a little dishwashing liquid. You can also take them some distance away and release them. One traditional way of

ABOVE *Gardeners seem more sympathetic to snails than to slugs, mainly because of their dainty shells, but they can be just as destructive. Hand-picking is the best way of reducing their numbers.*

BELOW *Birds can be welcome garden guests, but they can also be real pests. Protect crops, especially fruit, with nets.*

preventing slugs from approaching a plant is to surround it with sharp gravel or ashes.

Most mammals, such as rabbits and deer, can be kept away by fences. For rabbits, the fence needs to be dug into the soil at least 6 in. (15 cm) deep to prevent the animal from burrowing under it. Deer need a tall fence as they can jump to quite a height. These look ugly but can be covered with climbing plants. For mice and voles, use either traps which kill them or ones which capture them alive for subsequent release. Cats help to keep the problem at bay.

Cats and dogs can be pests. Your own dog can be trained, but keep the neighbor's out with a fence. Cats present a problem as they are difficult to train and they can climb fences. The best way of keeping the neighbor's cat out is to have one of your own, but this does not resolve the problem completely. There are cat deterrents, but they rarely seem to work. Perhaps the only solution is to create a litter tray away from the borders and beds, under shelter so that it is always dry, which will attract the cat.

Birds can be a nuisance as well as a help. Some remove buds from trees during the spring and fruit later in the season. The only way of dealing with this is to cover the crops with nets. However, do not leave these on all the time as birds also do a lot of good by eating insect pests.

PEST DETERRENTS

For centuries, growing different plants next to each other to deter pests has been common practice. Some of the claims made for these alternatives to pesticides are given here. Few have been scientifically proved, but it is worth experimenting to see whether they work under your conditions.

- **African marigold** Reduces nematodes

- **Anise** Deters aphids, fleas, and reduces numbers of cabbage worms

- **Borage** Reduces Japanese beetles and deters tomato horn worms

- **Caper spurge** Deters moles

- **Catnip** Deters ants, aphids, Colorado beetles, darkling beetles, flea beetles, Japanese beetles, squash bugs, and weevils

- **Celery** Deters cabbage butterflies

- **Chives** Good for rose black spot and deters Japanese beetles

- **Clover** Deters cabbage root flies

- **Cotton lavender** Deters corn wireworms and southern rootworms

- **Dill** Repels aphids and spider mites

- **Fennel** Deters aphids

- **French marigold** Deters Mexican bean beetles, nematodes

- **Garlic** General insect repellent

- **Hyssop** Repels flea beetles, decoys cabbage butterflies

- **Leek** Deters carrot root flies

- **Marigold** Reduces nematodes and cabbage pests

- **Mustard** Reduces aphids and decoys cabbage butterflies

- **Nasturtium** Reduces aphids, cabbage worms, Colorado beetles; deters squash bugs and whiteflies

- **Onion** Deters carrot root flies

- **Radish** Deters cucumber beetles, root flies, vine borers

- **Rosemary** Deters bean beetles, cabbage moths, carrot root flies

- **Rye** Reduces nematodes

- **Southernwood** Deters cabbage moths and carrot root flies

- **Tansy** Deters ants, aphids, cabbage worms, Colorado beetles, Japanese beetles, squash bugs

- **Thyme** Deters cabbage loopers, cabbage worms, whiteflies

- **Wormwood** Used as a general insecticide; deters mice and other rodents, slugs and snails

Garlic, a good insect repellant.

Leeks deter carrot root fly.

DISEASES

Much that has been said about pests also applies to diseases. Choose disease-resistant strains and consider some of the more traditional plants that have managed to survive because of their resistance. Again, many of the modern hybrids, especially flowers, have been bred for their appearance, often at the expense of toughness.

Diseases, like pests, often strike at one particular species and so the greater variety there is in a garden the more chance there is of the effects being contained. Good hygiene also helps. Remove all decaying or diseased matter as soon as you spot it. Check all plants which you bring into the garden and if any show signs of disease burn them immediately. Do not add diseased material to the compost heap.

RIGHT *The symptons of powdery mildew are dusty white patches on plants. Mildew, one of the most common diseases seen in gardens, can often be prevented by ensuring good air circulation around susceptible plants.*

RIGHT *Gray mold (Botrytis cinerea) causes leaves, stems and flowers to develop brown patches with a fluffy gray mold. Here we see the effects on chrysanthemums and primulas.*

FAR RIGHT *Leaf spot is the general name for a host of fungal infections that plague a wide range of plants.*

Some diseases are hosted by weeds; rust fungi live on groundsel (*Senecio vulgaris*), for example. Making sure that they do not grow in the garden reduces the chance of rust diseases. Another preventive measure can be taken against the mildews. These thrive on certain plants, such as asters, when they are planted so closely together that the air becomes stagnant. Giving this type of plant an open position with plenty of air circulating about it improves its chances.

Crops should be rotated so that they are not grown on the same soil two years running. This reduces the likelihood of disease building up in the soil. If plants have properly prepared and fed soil they will be strong and healthy, and much less prone to disease.

BELOW *Many diseases are hosted by weeds, for example, groundsel. Make sure all such plants are immediately eliminated from the garden.*

Following all this basic preventive advice will make life considerably easier for the gardener, but it is inevitable that certain diseases will enter the garden, especially the vegetable plot. Unfortunately, the commonest diseases, such as club root and potato blight, are difficult to treat, even with chemicals. The only solution is to burn the affected plants and use different ground for the next crop.

A range of organic fungicides can be used against certain diseases, such as mildews and molds, but many organic gardeners refuse to use them. If the garden is well run, and you are prepared to sacrifice for a season any part of a crop that is affected then they should not be necessary.

OTHER PROBLEMS

Not all problems are caused by pests and diseases. Sometimes weak or disfigured plants are caused by nutritional deficiencies. If the ground has been prepared properly with the incorporation of organic material then these should not occur. If deficiencies do occur they can be treated by the addition of one of the organic fertilizers that will supply whatever is missing. The cause of the deficiency can be determined either by observation of the plant or by soil analysis. The latter may the best way for the beginner.

NUTRITIONAL DEFICIENCIES

- **Magnesium** Leaves yellow, especially between the veins of older ones. *Apply seaweed in dried or liquid form.*

- **Nitrogen** Leaves become yellow, plant is stunted. *Use a fertilizer high in nitrogen, eg dried blood.*

- **Phosphorus** Older leaves turn blue, roots are underdeveloped. *Use a high phosphorus fertilizer, eg bone meal.*

- **Potassium** Leaves turn yellow around the edges, stunted plants, small flowers and fruit. *Use a high potassium fertilizer such as rock potash.*

---

5 THE VEGETABLE GARDEN

GROWING YOUR OWN VEGETABLES is one of the joys of gardening, bettered only by eating them. There are many reasons for growing them yourself. Unlike those brought from a grocery store, you have some idea as to what has gone into them and what has been sprayed onto them. They are tastier, as commercially grown crops are often bred to ensure that all mature at the same time or have skins which don't bruise easily, rather than for taste. Vegetables coming from the garden could not be fresher, and this also improves the taste. They are convenient; you do not have to go to the store when you need an extra couple of carrots. Finally, there is the sheer pleasure of growing them; dishes of your own vegetables are infinitely more satisfying than ones you have bought.

There is nothing difficult about growing vegetables. It just takes time and common sense. Prepare the ground well and tend the vegetables while they are growing and you will be repaid handsomely. The benefits will far outstrip the time and money you spend on raising them.

BELOW *Vegetable gardens do not have to be large to be successful. With careful planning even a small plot can generate a surprising quantity of vegetables and fruit during a year.*

PLANNING

Planning a vegetable garden is one of the most pleasurable of pastimes. During the heart of winter you can sit snugly indoors and browse through the seed catalogs, dreaming of what you will be growing and eating in the year to come.

The first step is to work out what you want to grow and how much of it. It is easy to get carried away and produce far too much. There is no point in growing three different varieties of pea if they are all going to mature around the same time (unless you are intending to freeze some). Similarly, when snap beans are ready to eat the kitchen often cannot keep up with them. On the other hand, if you produce a surplus you can give them away or sell them. Very few people will turn down the offer of fresh vegetables. A willing neighbor may well buy all your seeds for you in exchange for a regular supply of produce. This is unlikely to involve you in much extra work and you get yours free.

Having made out a realistic list of what vegetables you want to grow, the next step is to work out a sequence of sowings and harvestings so there is a constant supply, rather than having gluts and gaps alternating throughout the year. This is really something that you should keep constantly under review because there are some crops, such as garlic, that need planting before winter sets in for harvesting the next summer.

Also bear in mind that there will always be some crops overwintering in the ground. Unless the ground is permanently frozen, it is usual practice to leave parsnips, for example, where they grow until you are ready to eat them. Some greenstuff such as brussels sprouts and purple sprouting are also left where they are. So you will not be starting from a blank vegetable plot; there will be certain things to work around and to allow space for the next winter.

We have already touched upon the overall design of the garden and the position of the vegetable plot. This should be open, preferably with no overhanging trees, and on the best possible soil. The traditional vegetable garden is a rectangular plot with individual rows of

vegetables running across it. An alternative which many organic gardeners prefer is to create a series of raised beds, each holding one or more types of vegetable, planted in blocks rather than rows. A third possibility is a decorative one which is fast gaining in popularity. Here the vegetable garden is laid out as a parterre with the beds forming a decorative pattern. Within these the vegetables are also laid out in a decorative manner.

BELOW *With good planning and attention to your vegetables you can achieve row after row of healthy crops, with no need of artificial fertilizers and pesticides.*

43

All three layouts have their advocates and all are suitable for organic gardening. With rows it is possible to walk close to each line of vegetables, making it easier to attend to each plant and to weed between them. No space is lost through main paths. It is the most flexible of the three and easily allows for the different amount of space that each crop needs.

The raised bed system loses a lot of space to the paths between each. However, because the beds are never walked on, the soil is not compacted. The beds have to be relatively narrow so that you can reach the center. This normally means that the vegetables are planted in blocks, which does not always make for easy weeding, and numbers of individual crops may be restricted by the amount of space available in each bed. The beds can be raised either by using wooden planks or logs as supports or by sloping the sides. It is a useful system when the underlying soil is poor.

Parterres have few practical advantages, but they are extremely attractive. Their main disadvantage is that, as the vegetables are

planted in block patterns, the numbers grown are rather artificially controlled. Another disadvantage is that some gardeners are reluctant to allow vegetables to disappear to the kitchen as this ruins the pattern! Parterres have all the advantages of the raised bed, and in fact they are a form of the raised bed system, except that the beds are rarely rectangular. These are very attractive gardens and the ability to mix plants fits in well with the organic gardener's philosophy of companion planting.

One of the keys to achieving good crops is rotation. The idea is that you move the different vegetables around so that they do not come back to the same piece of ground for four years. This considerably reduces the risk of diseases building up and also allows for the right kind of soil preparation. Either create four individual plots, divide your one big plot into four or divide your individual raised beds into four groups. One is for permanent crops such as rhubarb, globe artichokes, and perennial herbs. The other three are rotated each year.

BELOW
Small beds can be arranged decoratively to create a pottager, a method of gardening which allows beneficial flowering plants to be incorporated into the scheme.

THREE YEAR ROTATION

A three-year rotational plan allows each plot three years' rest from a particular crop, thus reducing the chance of a buildup of disease.

PLOT 1
Single dig, add manure
Pea
Fava bean
Snap bean
Green bean
Navy bean
Onion
Leek
Celery
Corn
Tomato
Summer squash
Lettuce

PLOT 2
Single dig, add lime and organic fertilzers
Cabbage
Brussels sprout
Calabrese
Purple sprouting broccoli
Kale
Rutabaga
Turnip
Kohlrabi

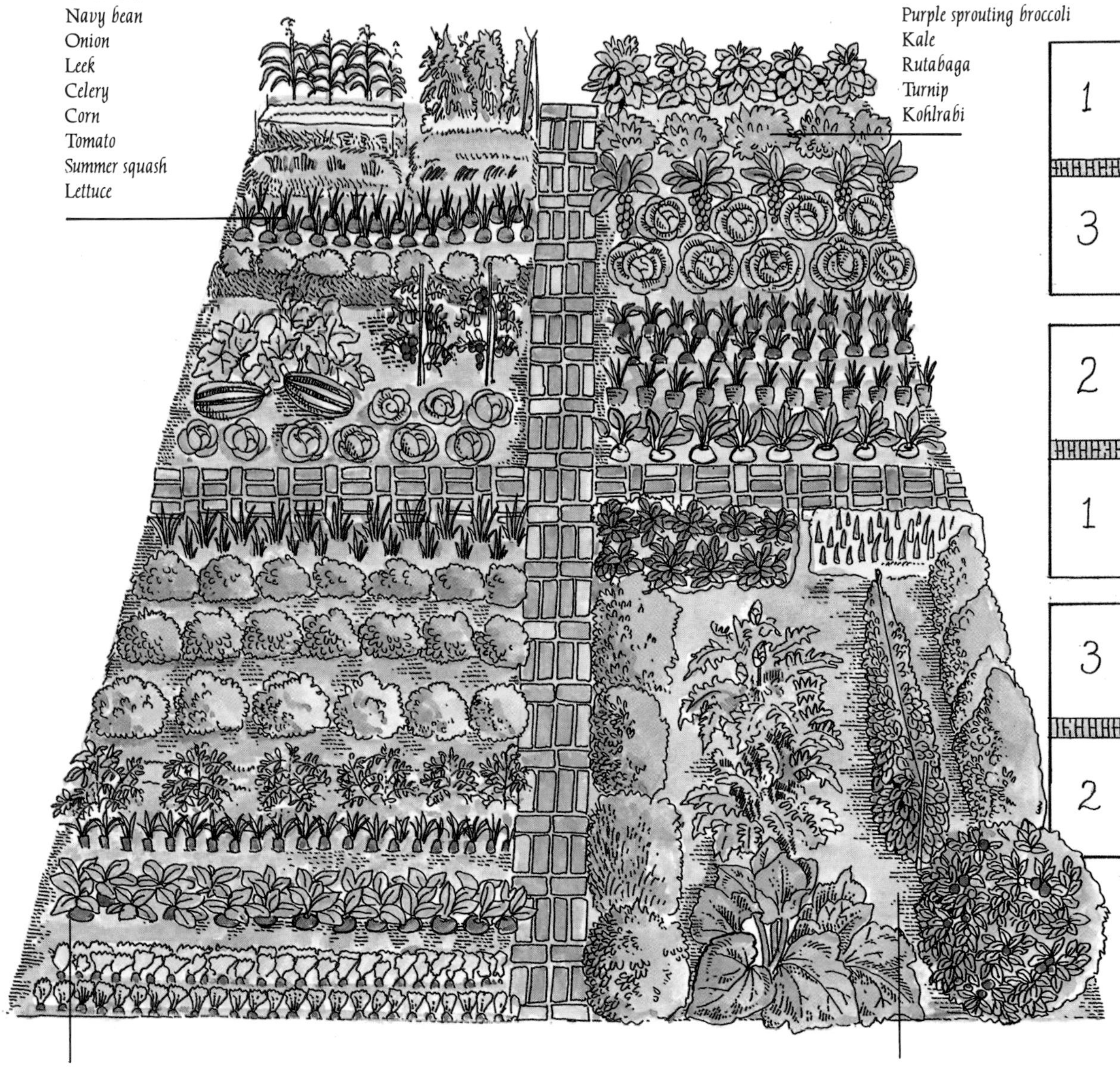

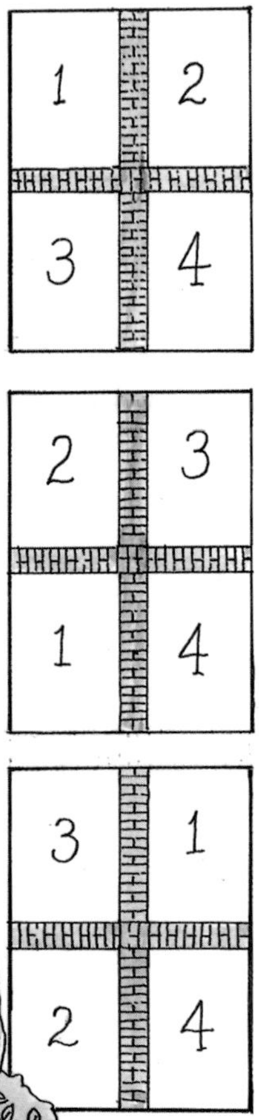

PLOT 3
Double dig, add manure
Potato
Parsnip
Beet
Carrot
Salsify
Scorzonera

PLOT 4
Permanent plot
Rhubarb
Asparagus
Artichoke
Jerusalem artichoke
Seakale
Perennial herbs
Fruit

ABOVE *There are various ways of maximizing space, an important consideration in small gardens. One method is to plant fast-growing crops, such as lettuce, between slower-growing ones – Brussels sprouts in this case. By the time the sprouts have grown to fill up the row, the lettuce will have been harvested.*

Individual types of vegetables can be grouped according to their nutritional needs and their hates. For example, it is best to keep lime away from potato crops, so on a three-year plan potatoes go on to a plot that was limed three years before when brassicas were on it. Rotations can vary according to the needs of the kitchen and the gardener. If there is enough space you can do a four-year rotation using five plots. This allows even longer for each plot to be rested from a particular crop.

Another feature of planning the cropping is to make the most use of space. Parsnips are slow germinating and it is usual practice to station sow these. In other words, three seeds are sown at 6 in. (15 cm) intervals. Radishes can be sown in the gaps between each station. These will germinate much faster than the parsnips and will mark the rows, making weeding easier. As they will be harvested before the parsnips start developing they will also make maximum use of what would otherwise have been unproductive soil. Sometimes you can plant a catch crop between rows of slower developing plants, for example, lettuce can be interplanted between rows of slower growing cabbages. As soon as one crop is harvested another should be put in its place. Thus leeks can follow early potatoes.

SOWING AND PLANTING

The soil should preferably be dug in the autumn (see pages 28–29). After a winter's weathering it should not be too difficult to break it down into a fine tilth suitable for sowing. Rake the bed level and remove any large stones or roots of weeds that surface.

The traditional way to sow is in rows. If the soil is dry it should be watered several hours before sowing so that the water has a chance to soak in. Using a garden line or string, or a long measuring stick, as a guide draw a straight furrow, or drill, with a pointed stick or the edge of a hoe. It should not be very deep; the planting depth of most vegetables is given on their package. Sow the seed thinly along the drill. Mark the ends of the row with sticks and rake the soil over the seeds, tamping it slightly with the back of the rake. Water dry ground.

For certain larger plants, such as parsnips, it is more economical in seed and effort to station sow. Two or three seeds are sown in groups at intervals equal to the plants' final distance apart. Once the seed has germinated, the strongest seedling is left and the rest weeded out. This saves sowing and weeding out all the intervening spaces.

The other method is to sow in blocks. You can make several short rows or scatter the seed over the whole area and rake it into the soil. Either way, the soil must be moist to trigger germination. Again, make certain that the seed is both marked and labelled.

If birds are likely to use the bed as a dust bath, or cats as a litter tray, cover it with a net until the seedlings are established. Keep well weeded, especially in the early stages. There should be no problem in distinguishing the vegetable seedlings, particularly if sown in rows. Most gardeners quickly learn to identify the different vegetables at their seedling stage, so that even scattered seed should not present a problem. If it does, use drills until you learn to recognize the young growth.

Some plants are better grown in pans or seed trays for later planting out. Most gardeners grow tomatoes, celery, celery root, and often brassicas in this way. Choose a good compost, either a loam-based or soil-less one depending on your preference. Fill the pot or tray with compost and settle it down by tapping it on the bench or lightly tamping it. Sow the seed thinly and cover lightly with compost. Keep the compost moist, but not over wet. Warmth will speed up germination. When the plants are big enough, repot into trays or individual pots. If the seed has been sown thinly enough you may be able to leave them in their original pots until it is time for transplanting. In this case they will need a liquid feed. Harden off by gradually introducing them to the ambient temperature.

Planting is best done on cool days, preferably when there is the possibility of light rain. Avoid hot sunny days. Cool moist conditions help the plant survive while its root system is unable to take up much water. After a few days the roots are again taking up the moisture that the plant requires. If the weather is dry, water the soil several hours before planting to allow it to soak in and then water again after

SOWING IN ROWS

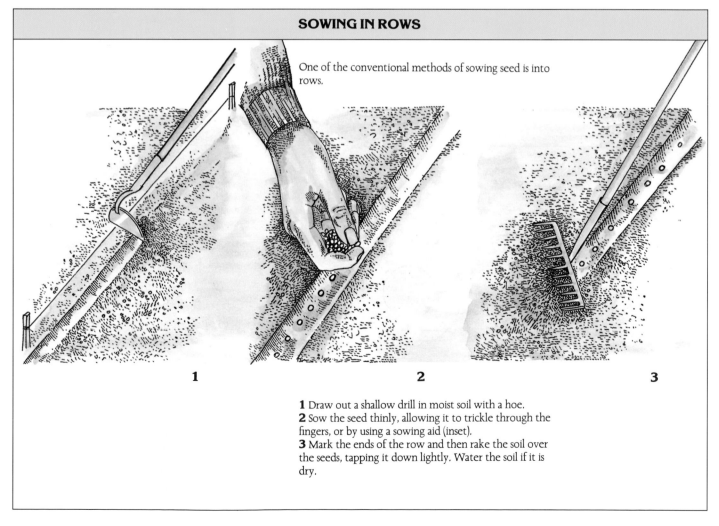

One of the conventional methods of sowing seed is into rows.

1 **2** **3**

1 Draw out a shallow drill in moist soil with a hoe.
2 Sow the seed thinly, allowing it to trickle through the fingers, or by using a sowing aid (inset).
3 Mark the ends of the row and then rake the soil over the seeds, tapping it down lightly. Water the soil if it is dry.

planting. Also water the plant in either its pot or nursery bed several hours before transplanting.

Dig a hole and insert the plant so it is at the same depth that it was in the nursery bed or pot. Firm the plant in. Brassicas need to be firmed in well; others, such as leeks, prefer the soil to be loose around them.

Many crops can be brought forward by sowing or planting under plastic or glass covers. These not only protect the plant from poor weather, but also warm up the soil.

TRAINING CLIMBING VEGETABLES

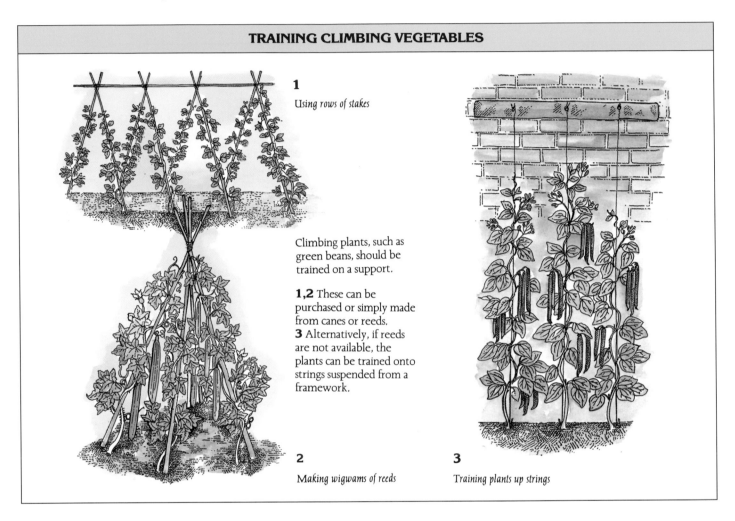

1
Using rows of stakes

Climbing plants, such as green beans, should be trained on a support.

1,2 These can be purchased or simply made from canes or reeds.
3 Alternatively, if reeds are not available, the plants can be trained onto strings suspended from a framework.

2
Making wigwams of reeds

3
Training plants up strings

CARE

Once seed has been sown or plants planted, make certain that weeds are kept at bay by hoeing or hand weeding, or by mulching. Do not work on the soil when it is wet as it can become compacted and the structure broken down.

Make certain that the plants have enough water for their needs. Plants can be watered individually with a watering pot, in which case make sure that they have enough and not just a trickle which only dampens the surface. An alternative is to use garden hose connected to a sprinkler which covers a wide area or trickle hose which allows water gently to ooze out of holes in the hose on to the ground. This is threaded between the plants so that water goes where it is needed. Unless there are problems with acid rain it is best to use rainwater. If you use domestic supply water it may be wise to run it into a reservoir beforehand, so that any chlorine can evaporate.

Once plants are in full growth they may well need feeding. The easiest method is to apply a liquid feed (see page 27). If you use organic fertilizers they will need to be watered in if no rain is imminent. Plants that are permanently in the ground, such as rhubarb or artichokes, can be top-dressed with compost or farmyard manure in the winter.

HARVESTING AND STORING

Few gardeners will have problems in knowing when vegetables are ready for use. Some, such as peas and beans, have a relatively short useful life and should be used as soon as possible. Any glut can either be given away or frozen. If you intend to collect your own seed, leave a few on the plant. Brassicas and root crops can be allowed to stay where they are until they are needed, even during the winter, as long as conditions are not too cold. In cold areas even these may be best harvested. Root crops, such as carrots, beet, and parsnips, can be stored in boxes of almost dry sand. They should be kept in a frost-free place. Brussels sprouts can be frozen. These and cabbages can be harvested on their stalks and hung upside down in a frost-free place.

Many gardeners collect their own seed. This is possible with most varieties, but with F₁ hybrids the chances are that the produce will not resemble the original. The easiest plants to collect seed from are the peas and beans. Allow some of the larger, fuller pods to remain on the plants until they have turned brown. Remove the seeds from the pods and dry them in the air. Store in paper bags in a cool, dry place. Other plants must be allowed to run to seed. This means keeping many plants for another season, as vegetables such as carrots and parsnips only flower in their second season. It is worth trying to save your own seed and, by careful selection, you can create a strain which suits your own tastes and garden conditions.

It is not only seed that can be saved for future crops, but also seed potatoes as well as bulbs of shallots and garlic. Some gardeners rarely have to buy any seed at all.

OVERLEAF *Onions and garlic can be attractively stored by tying the ends together to form "ropes". Hang them in a frost-free place and keep one or more ropes in the kitchen for day-to-day use. Cut off the onions as they are required.*

BELOW *Root crops can be over-wintered in a box of sand or peat, which should be just moist but not wet. Store in a frost-free environment.*

Individual Vegetables

Allium ampeloprasum
LEEK

Sow in nursery rows or trays and then transplant into holes made with a dibble. Reduce the length of the roots by about half and drop into the hole without refilling the soil. Fill the hole with water. Pull some soil up around the leeks as they grow to blanch the stem. The original planting can be in holes in a shallow trench which is gradually filled in. Leave in the open until required.

- **Soil** Rich in organic material
- **Site** Sunny and open
- **Sow** Early to mid spring
- **Plant** Early summer
- **Distance apart** 10 in. (25 cm)
- **Distance between rows** 12 in. (30 cm)
- **Harvest** Mid autumn onward
- **Pests** Onion flies

Allium ascalonicum
SHALLOTS

Plant as small bulbs. Early ones can be pulled and used as spring onions. As foliage dies back, break roots by gently lifting with a fork. Lift a week later and dry in a sunny position. Store in mesh bags in a frost-free place.

- **Soil** Well drained, fertile
- **Site** Open and sunny
- **Plant** Late winter and early spring
- **Distance apart** 9 in. (23 cm)
- **Distance between rows** 12 in. (30 cm)
- **Harvest** Late summer
- **Pests** Onion flies, onion eelworms, rot

Allium sativum
GARLIC

Plant individual cloves in early winter and overwinter in the open ground. Harvest in summer and allow to dry before tying into ropes or hanging in mesh bags. Store in a frost-free place.

- **Soil** Free draining, fertile
- **Site** Sunny and open
- **Plant** Late autumn or early winter; early spring
- **Distance apart** 6 in. (15 cm)
- **Distance between rows** 9 in. (23 cm)
- **Harvest** Mid summer
- **Pests** Rot

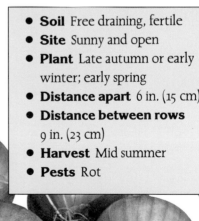

Allium cepa

ONION

Onions can be sown as seed or planted as sets, or small bulbs. Keep weeded. Harvest when the leaves turn brown and flop. Ease each with a fork to break the roots and lift about a week later. Dry in a sunny position. Tie into ropes or hang in mesh bags in a frost-free place.

- **Soil** Well drained, fertile
- **Site** Open and sunny
- **Sow** Early spring (winter under glass)
- **Plant** Late winter to early spring (sets and winter-sown seed)
- **Distance apart** 6 in. (15 cm)
- **Distance between rows** 12 in. (30 cm)
- **Harvest** Late summer onward
- **Pests** Onion flies, onion eelworms, rot

Allium cepa

GREEN ONIONS

Sow thinly in rows. Sow at three-week intervals for a succession. Hardy varieties can be sown in late summer for harvesting during winter. Covers may be needed for protection. Pull as required. Cannot be stored.

- **Soil** Well drained, fertile
- **Site** Open and sunny
- **Sow** Spring to mid summer (late winter under cover)
- **Distance between rows** 9 in. (23 cm)
- **Harvest** Spring onward
- **Pests** Onion flies, onion eelworms, rot

Apium graveolens

CELERY ROOT

This needs a long season, so start it under glass at about 60° F (15° C). It needs a moist soil so it benefits from plenty of organic material. Can be left in soil until needed or stored in just moist sand or peat.

- **Soil** Moisture retentive, rich in humus
- **Site** Open and sunny
- **Sow** Early spring
- **Plant** Late spring
- **Distance apart** 12 in. (30 cm)
- **Distance between rows** 15 in. (38 cm)
- **Harvest** Autumn onward
- **Pests** Carrot root flies, celery flies

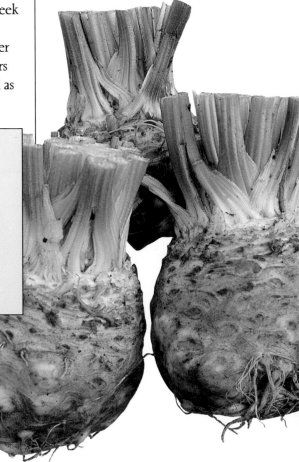

Apium graveolens

CELERY

This needs a long season, so start it under glass at about 60° F (15° C). Do not cover seed as they need light to germinate. It needs a moist soil so it benefits from plenty of organic material. Blanched varieties are planted in trenches and earthed up. Self-blanching varieties need to be grown in a block. Blanching varieties can be left covered up; use self-blanching varieties before serious frosts come.

- **Soil** Moisture retentive, rich in humus
- **Site** Open and sunny
- **Sow** Early spring
- **Plant** Late spring
- **Distance apart** 12 in. (30 cm)
- **Distance between rows** 15 in. (38 cm)
- **Harvest** Autumn onwards
- **Pests** Carrot root flies, celery flies

Asparagus officinalis

ASPARAGUS

This is a perennial crop. It can be grown from seed but plants can be inferior unless you use a reputable strain, so it is often best bought as crowns. It likes a rich soil. Dig a shallow trench with a ridge down the middle on which the crown sits. Spread the roots out and backfill. Keep well watered. Mulch with farmyard manure or compost in autumn after cutting back.

- **Soil** Well drained but rich
- **Site** Sunny
- **Sow** Spring
- **Plant** Spring
- **Distance apart** 18 in. (45 cm)
- **Distance between rows** 2 ft. (60 cm)
- **Harvest** Late spring or early summer
- **Pests** Slugs, asparagus rust

Beta vulgaris

BEETS

Beets are best grown rapidly and should not be allowed to dry out. Station sow. Sow at regular three-week intervals to ensure a succession. Lift in mid autumn and store in trays of almost dry sand or coir fiber.

- **Soil** Well prepared, rich, well drained
- **Site** Sunny
- **Sow** Early spring to mid summer
- **Distance apart** Thin to 4 in. (10 cm)
- **Distance between rows** 12 in. (30 cm)
- **Harvest** Early summer to late autumn
- **Pests** Aphids, beet leaf hoppers

53

Beta vulgaris

SWISS CHARD

Ruby chard is a red form of the same plant. Station sow. Pick young shoots regularly to get the best crop.

- **Soil** Moisture retentive, rich in organic material
- **Site** Open and sunny
- **Sow** Mid spring
- **Distance apart** 12 in. (30 cm)
- **Distance between rows** 15 in. (38 cm)
- **Harvest** Mid summer onward
- **Pests** Slugs

Brassica oleracea

BROCCOLI

Also known as purple sprouting. If the soil is acid, add lime to make it around pH 6.5. Sow in rows about 6 in. (15 cm) apart and transplant when about 5–6 in. (12.5–15 cm) high. Plant very firmly. Keep cutting once sprouting appears and do not allow to flower.

- **Soil** Well drained and rich
- **Site** Open and sunny
- **Sow** Mid spring to early summer
- **Plant** Early summer
- **Distance apart** 24 in. (60 cm)
- **Distance between rows** 24 in. (60 cm)
- **Harvest** Late winter to late spring
- **Pests** Caterpillars, cabbage root flies, club root, flea beetles

Brassica oleracea

BRUSSELS SPROUTS

If the soil is acid, add lime to make it around pH 6.5. Sow in rows about 6 in. (15 cm) apart and transplant when about 5–6 in. (12.5–15 cm) high. Plant very firmly. Sow in early spring under glass for an early autumn crop. Pick from the bottom while sprouts are still compact.

- **Soil** Well drained, rich
- **Site** Open and sunny
- **Sow** Early spring to early summer
- **Plant** Late spring to early summer
- **Distance apart** 30 in. (75 cm)
- **Distance between rows** 30 in. (75 cm)
- **Harvest** Early autumn to late winter
- **Pests** Caterpillars, cabbage root flies, club root, flea beetles

Brassica oleracea

CABBAGE

If the soil is acid, add lime to make it around pH 6.5. Sow in rows about 6 in. (15 cm) apart and transplant when about 5–6 in. (12.5–15 cm) high. Plant very firmly. Harvest when in season. Can be stored by hanging upside-down in a frost-free place.

SPRING CABBAGE

- **Soil** Well drained, rich
- **Site** Open and sunny
- **Sow** Late summer
- **Plant** Early autumn
- **Distance apart** 12–15 in. (30–38 cm)
- **Distance between rows** 18 in. (45 cm)
- **Harvest** Early to late spring
- **Pests** Caterpillars, cabbage root flies, club root, flea beetles

SUMMER CABBAGE

- **Soil** Well drained, rich
- **Site** Open and sunny
- **Sow** Mid spring
- **Plant** Late spring
- **Distance apart** 15 in. (38 cm)
- **Distance between rows** 18 in. (45 cm)
- **Harvest** Late summer to early autumn
- **Pests** Caterpillars, cabbage root flies, club root, flea beetles

Brassica oleracea

CALABRESE

If the soil is acid, add lime to make it around pH 6.5. Calabrese do not like to be disturbed so sow in rows where they are to grow. Station sow at 12 in. (30 cm) intervals. Keep cutting once sprouting appears and do not allow to flower.

- **Soil** Well drained, rich
- **Site** Open and sunny
- **Sow** Mid spring to early summer
- **Distance apart** 12 in. (30 cm)
- **Distance between rows** 12 in. (30 cm)
- **Harvest** Late summer to autumn
- **Pests** Caterpillars, cabbage root flies, club root, flea beetles

Brassica oleracea

CAULIFLOWER

If the soil is acid, add lime to make it around pH 6.5. Sow in rows about 6 in. (15 cm) apart and transplant when about 5–6 in. (12.5–15 cm) high. Sow summer varieties under glass in mid winter. Plant very firmly. Harvest when heads are firm. Can be stored by hanging upside-down in a frost-free place.

- **Soil** Well drained, rich
- **Site** Open and sunny
- **Sow** Early to late spring
- **Plant** Mid spring to early summer
- **Distance apart** 24 in. (60 cm)
- **Distance between rows** 24 in. (60 cm)
- **Harvest** Summer or autumn
- **Pests** Caterpillars, cabbage root flies, club root, flea beetles

WINTER AND RED CABBAGE

- **Soil** Well drained, rich
- **Site** Open and sunny
- **Sow** Late spring
- **Plant** Early summer
- **Distance apart** 18 in. (45 cm)
- **Distance between rows** 18 in. (45 cm)
- **Harvest** Autumn onward
- **Pests** Caterpillars, cabbage root flies, club root, flea beetles

Brassica oleracea

KALE

If the soil is acid, add lime to make it around pH 6.5. Sow in rows about 6 in. (15 cm) apart and transplant when about 5–6 in. (12.5–15 cm) high. Plant very firmly. Harvest by picking a few of the young leaves off each plant.

- **Soil** Well drained, rich soil
- **Site** Open and sunny
- **Sow** Early to late spring
- **Plant** Mid spring to early summer
- **Distance apart** 18 in. (45 cm)
- **Distance between rows** 18 in. (45 cm)
- **Harvest** Late autumn onward
- **Pests** Caterpillars, cabbage root flies, club root, flea beetles

Brassica oleracea

KOHLRABI

Although it looks like a root crop this is one of the cabbage family and must be treated as such. Sow seed where the plants are to crop. Will stand drought reasonably well. Harvest while small, just 2 in. (5 cm), and tender. Store for a short time in just moist sand or peat in a frost-free place.

- **Soil** Light rich soil
- **Site** Open and sunny
- **Sow** Mid spring to mid summer
- **Distance apart** 6 in. (15 cm)
- **Distance between rows** 9 in. (23 cm)
- **Harvest** Early summer onward
- **Pests** Cabbage root flies, flea beetles

Brassica rapa

TURNIP

Soil must not become too dry for the best crops. Can be sown in late winter under cover for early crops. They are best when quite small. Can be left in the ground until required or stored in just moist peat or sand.

- **Soil** Moisture retentive, rich in organic material
- **Site** Sunny and open
- **Sow** Mid spring to mid summer
- **Distance apart** 8 in. (20 cm)
- **Distance between rows** 12 in. (30 cm)
- **Harvest** Summer onward
- **Pests** Flea beetles, cabbage root flies, turnip weevil

Brassica rutabaga

RUTABAGA

Do not use ground previously used for brassicas. Sow where plants are to crop. Do not allow soil to become too dry. Can be left in the ground until required or stored in boxes of just moist peat or sand.

- **Soil** Well drained
- **Site** Open and sunny
- **Sow** Late spring or early summer
- **Distance apart** 12 in. (30 cm)
- **Distance between rows** 15 in. (38 cm)
- **Harvest** Mid autumn onward
- **Pests** Club root, cabbage root flies, flea beets, turnip weevils

Capsicum annuum

PEPPER

Peppers may need to be covered in colder areas. Sow under glass at about 60° F (15° C) and transplant into the open when frosts have passed. Tie in to poles for support. Pinch out growing tips at 6 in. (15 cm). Feed with liquid seaweed once fruit starts to swell.

- **Soil** Moisture retentive
- **Site** Sheltered and sunny
- **Sow** Late winter
- **Plant** Late spring
- **Distance apart** 24 in. (60 cm)
- **Distance between rows** 24 in. (60 cm)
- **Harvest** Late summer onward
- **Pests** Aphids, red spider mites, slugs

Cucumis sativus

CUCUMBER

Outside cucumbers can be grown on the ground or tied up poles. Start seed off under glass at about 60° F (15° C) or *in situ* under a glass jar or cover. Do not plant out before last frosts. Pick regularly to encourage more to form. Never let them dry out. Cannot be stored except for small ones (gherkins), which can be pickled.

- **Soil** Well manured
- **Site** Sunny
- **Sow** Mid spring (inside), late spring (outside)
- **Plant** Late spring, early summer
- **Distance apart** 30 in. (75 cm)
- **Distance between rows** 36 in. (90 cm)
- **Harvest** Summer onward to first frosts
- **Pests** Cucumber beetles, cucumber mosaic virus, slugs

Cucurbita spp

ZUCCHINI, SUMMER SQUASH, PUMPKIN, SQUASH

Zucchini are really only immature squashes, although there is seed specifically bred for producing them. They are both grown in the same way. Start seed off under glass at around 60° F (15° C) or *in situ* covered with a glass jar or cover. Do not plant out before last frosts. Pick zucchini regularly to encourage more to form. Pumpkins and squashes can be stored for a while in frost-free conditions. Zucchini can be frozen.

- **Soil** Rich, moisture retentive
- **Site** Sunny and open
- **Sow** Mid spring (inside), late spring or early summer (outside)
- **Plant** Late spring or early summer
- **Distance apart** 3 ft. (90 cm) (bush), 4 ft. (120 cm) (trailing)
- **Distance between rows** 4 ft. (120 cm)
- **Harvest** Mid summer until first frosts
- **Pests** Aphids, slugs, squash vine borers, cucumber beetles

Cynara scolymus

ARTICHOKE

The piece that is eaten is the heart of the flower head. It is planted as a permanent crop on well-manured soil. Seed-produced plants are usually inferior, so grow from rooted suckers (offsets). Cut heads while they are still tight. Only harvest up to six heads per plant; remove all other buds. Replace a third of the crop each year from rooted cuttings.

- **Soil** Rich in organic material, well drained
- **Site** Sunny and sheltered
- **Plant** Spring
- **Distance apart** 36 in. (90 cm)
- **Distance between rows** 36 in. (90 cm)
- **Harvest** Summer
- **Pests** Slugs, aphids

Daucus carota v. sativum

CARROT

Carrots can be sown earlier under cover or in cold frames to be harvested mid spring. Sow thinly and successively at three-week intervals. Organic material in soil must be well rotted. Thin in damp weather and remove thinnings. Store over winter in just moist sand or peat in a frost-proof place.

- **Soil** Light soil with well-rotted compost
- **Site** Open and sunny
- **Sow** Early spring to mid summer
- **Distance apart** Thin to 3 in. (7.5 cm)
- **Distance between rows** 6 in. (15 cm)
- **Harvest** Early summer onward
- **Pests** Carrot root flies, slugs

Helianthus tuberosus

JERUSALEM ARTICHOKE

Plant in a trench at about 6 in. (15 cm) deep. Cut stems down in autumn but leave the tubers in the soil until required. Make certain that every one is removed from the soil or they will sprout again. This is not such a problem if the same site is used each year (which it can for this crop).

- **Soil** Rich in organic material
- **Site** Open and sunny
- **Plant** Late winter to early spring
- **Distance apart** 15 in. (38 cm)
- **Distance between rows** 36 in. (90 cm)
- **Harvest** Mid autumn onward
- **Pests** Usually trouble free

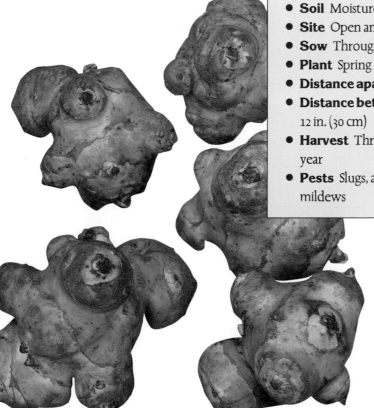

Lactuca sativa

LETTUCE

Lettuce can be grown throughout the year, depending on the varieties. They are good as catch crops. Most summer sowings are best thinned rather than transplanted. Early sowings can be under cover and winter varieties can be overwintered under cover.

- **Soil** Moisture retentive
- **Site** Open and sunny
- **Sow** Throughout the year
- **Plant** Spring
- **Distance apart** 9 in. (23 cm)
- **Distance between rows** 12 in. (30 cm)
- **Harvest** Throughout the year
- **Pests** Slugs, aphids, rot, and mildews

Lycopersicon esculentum

TOMATO

Sow seed inside and transplant seedlings to individual pots. Plant out after last frosts. Tie to poles (except bush varieties) and regularly pinch out side shoots (except bush varieties). Feed every two weeks with liquid seaweed after fruit start to swell. Cover at the end of autumn to extend the season.

- **Soil** Moisture retaining, organically rich
- **Site** Sunny
- **Sow** Early to mid spring (inside)
- **Plant** Late spring to early summer
- **Distance apart** 24 in. (60 cm)
- **Distance between rows** 24 in. (60 cm)
- **Harvest** Summer onward
- **Pests** Aphids, red spider mites, blight, blossom end rot, virus diseases

Pastinaca sativa

Parsnip

If manure is added to the soil it must be well rotted. Seed is slow to germinate. Station sow seed with a few radishes in the intervening spaces to mark the row. Make individual holes with a crowbar in stony ground and fill with compost. Parsnip taste sweeter after frosts have started. Can be left in the ground or stored in just damp sand or peat.

- **Soil** Fertile
- **Site** Open and sunny
- **Sow** Early to mid spring
- **Distance apart** 9 in. (23 cm)
- **Distance between rows** 12 in. (30 cm)
- **Harvest** Autumn onward
- **Pests** Carrot root flies, parsnip canker

Phaseolus multiflorus

Green beans

These can be grown in the same place each year. Dig in plenty of fibrous organic material deep down to ensure that moisture is retained. Sow inside or *in situ*. Support with reeds, poles, or strings. Can be sown in double rows 24 in. (60 cm) apart or in a circle using a wigwam support. Can be frozen or canned for storing.

- **Soil** Plenty of organic matter at the roots
- **Site** Open and sunny
- **Sow** Late spring to early summer
- **Plant** Late spring to early summer
- **Distance apart** 10 in. (25 cm)
- **Distance between rows** 36 in. (90 cm)
- **Harvest** Mid summer to mid autumn
- **Pests** Aphids, slugs, bean weevils

Phaseolus vulgaris

French beans

Also known as dwarf beans. Can be Also known as snap beans. Can be sown in double rows in shallow trenches, 2 in. (5 cm) deep. Climbing varieties are sown one or two to a cane and thinned to one plant. Some varieties need support. Many varieties can be frozen or shelled and dried.

- **Soil** Any good garden soil
- **Site** Open and sunny
- **Sow** Early spring to early summer
- **Distance apart** 4 in. (10 cm)
- **Distance between rows** 12 in. (30 cm)
- **Harvest** Early summer to mid autumn
- **Pests** Aphids, slugs, bean weevils

Pisum sativum

Pea

Sow two rows in a shallow trench. Rows should be the same distance apart as the eventual height of the row. Protect from bird attack with nets in the early stages. Taller peas will need support from sticks or nets. Weed carefully so as not to disturb the roots. Can be stored by drying or freezing.

- **Soil** Average garden soil
- **Site** Open and sunny
- **Sow** Early spring to mid summer
- **Distance apart** 2 in. (5 cm)
- **Distance between rows** Same as height of row
- **Harvest** Early summer onward
- **Pests** Birds, mice, mildew, pea moths

Raphanus salivus

Radish

Sow at regular intervals to ensure a succession. Can be used as a catch crop or intercrop. The first sowing can be in late winter under cover. Ensure that they never dry out. Use radishes before they get too old. Winter varieties can be stored in just damp peat or sand.

- **Soil** Any good garden soil
- **Site** Sunny and open
- **Sow** Early spring onwards
- **Distance between rows** 8 in. (20 cm)
- **Harvest** Spring onward
- **Pests** Flea beetles, slugs

Rheum rhaponticum

Rhubarb

This is kept on a permanent site, which should be well prepared with organic material and heavily mulched with farmyard manure or compost each winter. Crowns can be divided with a spade. An early crop can be forced by covering the crown with a bucket or something similar. Harvest by pulling stalks out of their socket. Can be frozen.

- **Soil** Moisture retentive, enriched with organic material
- **Site** Open and sunny
- **Plant** Spring
- **Distance apart** 36 in. (90 cm)
- **Distance between rows** 36 in. (90 cm)
- **Harvest** Early spring to mid summer
- **Pests** Apids, viral diseases

Solanum melongena v. esculentum

EGGPLANT

A perennial in warmer climates, annual in colder ones. Sow seed inside in early spring and plant out later in spring, with protective cover in colder areas. Tie plants firmly to stakes. Do not allow to dry out. Feed with liquid manure or seaweed.

- **Soil** Average loam, rich in organic material
- **Site** Sunny and sheltered
- **Sow** Early spring (inside)
- **Plant** Mid to late spring
- **Distance apart** 24 in. (60 cm)
- **Distance between rows** 24 in. (60 cm)
- **Harvest** While skins are shiny
- **Pests** Aphids, Colorado beetles, flea beetles

Solanum tuberosum

POTATO

Put seed potatoes in a cool, light spot to produce shoots. Dig a trench, put potatoes 12 in. (30 cm) apart and re-cover. Draw up a slight mound and continue to pull this up as the plant grows. Lift and leave to dry for a few hours before storing. Store in paper or burlap sacks in a frost-free place.

- **Soil** Rich in organic material and water retentive
- **Site** Sunny and open
- **Plant** Early to late spring
- **Distance apart** 12 in. (30 cm)
- **Distance between rows** 24 in. (60 cm)
- **Harvest** Early summer onward
- **Pests** Blight, Colorado beetles, scab, wireworms

Spinacia oleracea

SPINACH

The soil must not be too hot and dry otherwise the spinach bolts. Sow every four weeks to ensure a succession. Pick regularly. Can be frozen.

- **Soil** Moisture retentive, rich in organic material
- **Site** Light but not too sunny
- **Sow** Early spring to mid summer
- **Plant** Early spring from a mid-winter sowing
- **Distance apart** 6 in. (15 cm)
- **Distance between rows** 12 in. (30 cm)
- **Harvest** Late spring onward
- **Pests** Aphids, slugs

Tragopogon porrifolius

SALSIFY

Soil for salsify should be enriched with organic material that has been well rotted. Station sow the seed. Can be left in the ground until required or stored in trays of just moist peat or sand. Scorzonera is grown in the same way.

- **Soil** Deeply prepared, with organic material
- **Site** Open and sunny
- **Sow** Early spring
- **Distance apart** 6 in. (15 cm)
- **Distance between rows** 12 in. (30 cm)
- **Harvest** Mid autumn onward
- **Pests** Trouble free

Vicia faba

FAVA BEANS

Sow two rows in a shallow trench, 2 in. (5 cm) deep. For early crops, sow in late autumn and overwinter under cover. Pinch out tops to prevent pests when first pods appear. Can be stored by freezing.

- **Soil** Any average garden soil
- **Site** Open and sunny
- **Sow** Late autumn or late winter
- **Distance apart** 4 in. (10 cm)
- **Distance between rows** 36 in. (90 cm)
- **Harvest** Early summer to early autumn
- **Pests** Pea weevils, bean weevils

Zea mays v. rugosa

CORN

Sweetcorn can be sown inside under gentle heat at 60° F (15° C) and planted out or sown *in situ*. It is best planted in blocks which ensures better pollination. Corn is shallow rooted so deter weeds with mulch rather than by hoeing. Store by freezing.

- **Soil** Moisture retentive
- **Site** Sunny
- **Sow** Mid spring
- **Plant** Late spring
- **Distance apart** 24 in. (60 cm)
- **Harvest** Late summer onward
- **Pests** Corn smut

6 THE FRUIT GARDEN

HE TASTE OF FRUIT THAT has come straight from the plant cannot be bettered. Supermarkets and grocery stores put uniformity of shape, an unblemished appearance, and ability to travel without getting bruised way before taste and many of our best loved and most flavorsome apples, for example, have all but disappeared because of this approach. Fortunately, the organic gardener can choose what plants he or she likes.

Fruiting plants can take up a lot of space and you may feel that their short fruiting season does not justify the amount of ground they occupy. However, during their brief period of glory they are worth their weight in gold, especially as any surplus can be frozen, canned, or juiced. Fruit has been grown in gardens since medieval times and it was as much for the production of drinks as for fresh fruit that they were first introduced.

As so much fruit is eaten fresh, often straight from the plant, it is important that as few sprays and other chemicals as possible are used. As with vegetables, good housekeeping and vigilance will help to keep pests and diseases under control.

RIGHT Not only humans love these luscious strawberries: remove slugs by hand and erect nets to foil marauding birds. Straw helps to keep the fruit off the ground, preventing it from getting dirty and rotting.

SOFT FRUIT

Soft fruits are the quickest way to get established. Many will be producing fruit within a year or so of planting.

SOIL AND SITE

The site for fruit should be open, so that plenty of air circulates, but sheltered against strong winds. Fruiting plants will be in the same position for several years, so it is essential to prepare the ground thoroughly. Remove all perennial weeds at this stage; it is very difficult to extract any which re-emerge around the base of a prickly gooseberry bush, for example. Then double dig the soil and add plenty of organic material to it, preferably in the autumn so that the winter's weather can break it down. This allows time for any odd pieces of weed shoot to re-emerge so that the soil can be cleared completely.

PLANTING

Whether the plants are herbaceous (strawberries), pole (raspberries), or bush (currants) they should be planted at the same depth as they were in their pots or nursery beds. Do not plant in hot dry weather. Water in well.

AFTERCARE

Keep the site weed free and watered. Apply rock potash or dried seaweed in spring. Keep plants in shape by pruning in late winter or early spring. Mulch to retain moisture and keep weeds down; a winter mulch of well rotted farmyard manure or compost is beneficial. Pick fruit as it ripens and remove any that is rotting.

TRAINING

Remove stawberry runners and use them to start new rows. Cut out the current year's raspberry poles after fruiting and tie in the new poles where they cross the horizontal wires. Cut out excess poles. Treat blackberries and loganberries in the same way, training the long briars along the horizontal wires. Gooseberries, red currants, and white currants are all trained as open bushes or flat against a support as cordons. For open bushes, cut back the leaders in spring to about half of that year's growth and the laterals to about 3 in. (7.5 cm).

After about three years, cut out some of the older main shoots, allowing them to be replaced by new growth, and cut laterals back to about 1 in. (2.5 cm) of the current year's growth. Cordons can be trained as for tree fruit (see page 68). Black currants only need to have any weak growth removed for the first couple of years and thereafter about a quarter of the old branches should be cut out from the base during late summer. Blueberries need to have the bush kept open by taking out a few of the older stems in spring to prevent overcrowding and to stimulate new growth.

ABOVE *Pole fruit, such as these raspberries, need to be tied to some form of support. Two or three taut wires are usually sufficient to stop the canes flopping over or moving around in the wind.*

SOFT FRUIT						
Plant	**Type**	**Height**	**Planting distance**	**Fruiting season**	**Cropping age**	**Special needs**
Black currant	Bush	5 ft. (150 cm)	5 ft. (150 cm)	Summer	2 years	High nitrogen requirement
Blackberry	Briar	6 ft. (180 cm)	10 ft. (3 m)	Autumn	1 year	Tying to wires
Blueberry	Bush	5 ft. (150 cm)	5 ft. (150 cm)	Summer	1–2 years	Soil ph 4.5–5.0
Gooseberry	Bush	5 ft. (150 cm)	5 ft. (150 cm)	Summer	2 years	Moisture retentive soil
Gooseberry	Cordon	4 ft. (120 cm)	1–3 ft. (30–90 cm)	Summer	2 years	Moisture retentive soil
Loganberry	Briar	6 ft. (180 cm)	10 ft. (3 cm)	Autumn	1 year	Tying to wires
Raspberry	Cane	6 ft. (180 cm)	18 in. (45 cm)	Summer onward	1 year	Supporting the poles
Red currant	Bush	5 ft. (150 cm)	5 ft. (150 cm)	Summer	2 years	Well drained soil
Red currant	Cordon	4 ft. (120 cm)	1–3 ft. (30–90 cm)	Summer	2 years	Well drained soil
Strawberry	Non-woody plants	10 in. (25 cm)	18 in. (45 cm)	Early summer onward	1 year	
White currant	Bush	5 ft. (150 cm)	5 ft. (150 cm)	Summer	2 years	Well drained soil
White currant	Cordon	4 ft. (120 cm)	1–3 ft. (30–90 cm)	Summer	2 years	Well drained soil

PESTS AND DISEASES

Well cared for and vigorous plants are the best insurance against disease. Putting straw under the strawberry plants will keep them off the ground and help air to circulate, reducing the incidence of mildew and botrytis. These two diseases can also affect other fruiting plants but by keeping the plants reasonably open and not too close together air can circulate, reducing the risk.

Birds, one of the biggest pests, can be stopped by covering the plants with nets. Either net individual rows or create a complete enclosure. Only net the plants when they are in fruit and possibly earlier, when they are in bud, if there is a problem with birds stripping them. For the rest of the year birds should be allowed free access as they reduce the number of pests.

Aphids can be a problem if not kept under control. Plant plenty of flowers nearby to encourage ladybugs, hoverflies, and lacewings, which will normally reduce aphid populations to acceptable levels. If there is a sudden outbreak, wash them off with a water spray or use a soft soap spray, but only spray the affected areas. Slugs can be a problem on strawberries and should be picked off by hand.

Raspberry beetles can be a nuisance as their grubs can be found in the ripening fruit. There is no effective way of coping with this other than hoeing around the base of the plants several times during the winter to bring the pupa to the surface. An alternative is to use a spray such as one containing derris which should be applied just before the fruit ripens. Avoid spraying when bees are in the area.

~ TREE FRUIT ~

Apples spring immediately to mind when thinking of tree fruit, but there is a very wide range of other fruit including plums, green-gages, pears, quinces, mulberries, cherries, peaches, apricots, walnuts, filberts, and figs. Most are hardy and will produce fruit every year. Some, such as figs, need a warmer climate, although they can be fruited against a warm wall.

BELOW *Fruit trees can be grown free-standing, like the plum shown here, or trained against a wall or along wires. The first method takes up more space, but is likely to produce a larger yield.*

TRAINING A CORDON

Cordonned fruit trees have the advantage of taking up little space, allowing several varieties to be grown along a wall or fence.

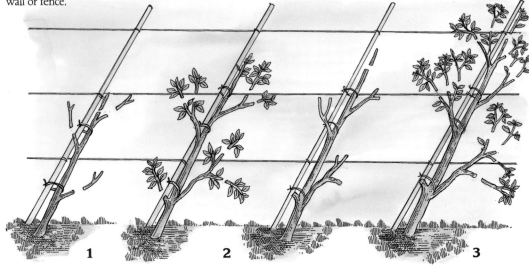

Double Cordon

Triple Cordon **4**

1 After planting the leading shoot should be cut back by about a third.

2 At the same time any side-shoots should be cut back to a bud about 2–3 in. (5–7.5 cm) from the main stem. Subsequent pruning should again cut back any new side shoots to the same length and the new growth on any existing ones to about 1 in. (2.5 cm).

3 Cut back the new growth of the main shoot by about a third each time until it has reached the top of the pole against which it is trained.

4 It is possible to create double to triple cordons by allowing the bottom shoots to grow in the same manner.

TRAINING AN ESPALIER

Espalier trees are more productive than cordons and can look very attractive.

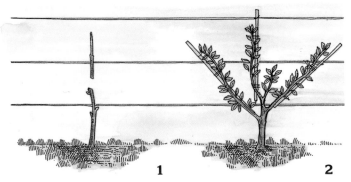

1 After planting, prune back to the bottom three good buds.

2 In the spring tie the bottom two shoots to poles held at about 45 degrees and remove any new side shoots that might appear.

3 In the second winter remove about a third of the year's new growth on the lower shoots and pull them down to the bottom wires. The main shoot should be pruned back to three good buds which will form the next layer.

4 During the ensuing summer cut back all new side shoots to about 1–3 in. (2–7.5 cm) and the growth on any existing side shoots to about 1 in. (2.5 cm).

5 Repeat this process until the height and width has been achieved. Thereafter keep cutting back secondary growth to about 1 in. (2.5 cm).

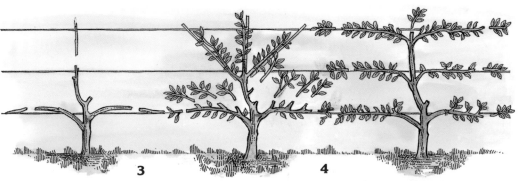

SOIL AND SITE

As for soft fruit, you need to prepare the soil well by removing weeds and incorporating well rotted organic material, both to act as a feed and to retain moisture. Incorporate organic material into the surrounding area, well beyond the immediate planting hole.

PLANTING

Plant in winter, to the same depth that the tree or bush was in the pot or nursery bed. Water in well. For free-standing trees insert a short stake before planting and tie the base of the tree to it. This allows the top to move freely but keeps the roots anchored. Cordons or espaliers need a wall or framework.

AFTERCARE

Watering is particularly important just as the fruit begins to swell. Water the whole area covered by the tree. Feed by adding a mulch of well rotted manure or compost in winter. Alternatively, you can apply a spring feed of seaweed.

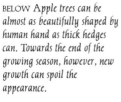

BELOW *Apple trees can be almost as beautifully shaped by human hand as thick hedges can. Towards the end of the growing season, however, new growth can spoil the appearance.*

POLLINATION

Some fruit trees, such as apples and cherries, are not self-fertile; in other words, they need a different type of tree to fertilize the flowers. In many areas there are enough types available in neighbors' gardens and farms. Where there are no other fruit trees around, check with your supplier as to which trees are compatible and always grow at least in pairs.

PRUNING AND TRAINING

Keep fruit trees as open as possible to allow the sunlight to reach the fruit and also to allow air to circulate. A variety of shapes can be adopted (see below).

PESTS AND DISEASES

Again, good husbandry will reduce the incidence of pests and diseases, and the damage that they cause. Many of the pests affecting trees lie dormant in the soil during the winter, so turn the soil over several times to expose them to birds and other predators. Apply grease bands around the trunks to trap insects as they crawl back up the trees in spring. Birds can be a nuisance and if you grow the trees on dwarfing rootstocks, you can cover them in net or grow them in a cage. For taller trees, little can be done.

Apples suffer from the grubs of codling moths. You can catch the moths using pheromone traps which exude the smell of the female moth and then trap the males on a sticky paper, reducing the chances of fertilization. The worse disease is fire blight, in which the trees look as though they have been burnt. Nothing can be done except to burn the trees immediately.

LEFT By using small or trained trees, fruit can be successfully mixed into the aesthetically appealing heart of a garden. Here, pears flourish in a parterre.

RIGHT Plums, those most delicious of fruits, are quite straightforward to grow. Pruning should be kept to a minimum, however, as they suffer from silver leaf, which is contracted through wounds.

FRUIT TREE FORMS

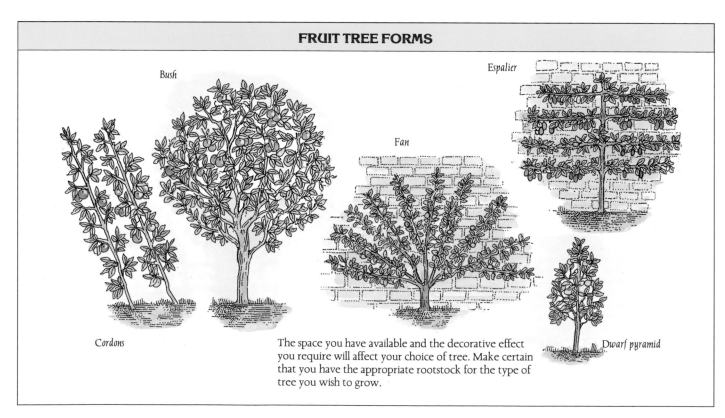

Bush

Espalier

Fan

Cordons

Dwarf pyramid

The space you have available and the decorative effect you require will affect your choice of tree. Make certain that you have the appropriate rootstock for the type of tree you wish to grow.

THE HERB GARDEN

ERBS WERE AMONG THE earliest plants to be grown in the garden. Until relatively recently they played a much greater part in our domestic economy. They were used to flavor foods, to cure ailments to disguise smells, and to act as insect repellents.

Culinary usage is still very important and it is for this reason that most herbs are still grown in the garden. Increasingly, though, people are turning to herbal remedies and rejecting synthetic drugs. Fumigants are not quite as important as they were but many people still use them around the house, and there is a world of difference between the smells produced by natural herbs and the synthetic ones from an aerosol. The use of potpourri and dried herbs is on the increase. Very few people strew herbs on the floor to repel fleas, but they are still to be found hanging up in the cupboards of many country cottages.

RIGHT *Fresh herbs bring a natural zest to the kitchen, but are doubly useful to an organic garden as many of them attract beneficial insects. Here they are grown in a special herb knot garden, with partitions of box hedging.*

PLANNING

Herbs are not the easiest of plants to design with. Most people have romantic ideas of herb gardens but they are extremely difficult to plan effectively and are quite difficult to keep looking attractive.

Many gardeners prefer to keep them mixed into the flower or vegetable borders, for several reasons. On the whole, herbs are not very beautiful plants and a mass planting can be quite dull. Mixing them in with other plants overcomes this problem. Many are very attractive to bees and all the insects that are beneficial to a garden, such as lacewings and hoverflies. Putting them among flowers and vegetables helps to reduce the number of pests. If not concentrated in one area, a few of the important ones, such as the mints, can be put near the kitchen door, handy when they are required.

Having said all this, there is no reason why gardeners should not create a herb garden. Bear in mind when designing it that the early part of the season is fine, but in time many plants grow leggy and start to flop over their neighbors. One way to cope with this is to make a series of small borders, on the basis of a parterre (see pages 43–44) or a knot garden. One popular method is to use a wagonwheel and plant up each segment with a different herb. As all herbs should be readily accessible, consider laying out a square terrace of concrete slabs with every other one missing, much in the style of a chess- or checker-board. Then plant each square of earth with a different herb. Nearly all herbs prefer a warm sunny site.

DIFFERENT STYLES OF HERB GARDEN

Herbs can be grown in a wide variety of ways, and here are just a few suggestions for designs.

Knot Herb Garden Parterre

Formal Herb Garden

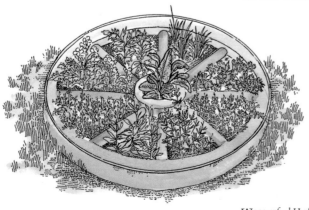

Wagonwheel Herb Garden

73

INDIVIDUAL HERBS

BASIL A perennial which is grown mainly as an annual as it succumbs to frost. It prefers a sheltered site. Sow under glass in early spring and plant out after frosts have passed. The leaves can be dried or frozen. It deters flies and is often planted as a companion to tomatoes.

BAY A shrubby perennial which is not hardy in cold districts. It can be grown in containers in these areas. It prefers a rich, well drained soil in light shade or full sun. Dry the leaves. It is used in small amounts in cooking.

BORAGE An attractive bushy annual which likes an open, sunny position. It will normally self-sow and after initial sowing need never be sown again. It does well in flower borders and bees love it. Sow in spring.

CHIVES A decorative perennial which does well in ornamental borders. It is a bulb and should be planted in spring. The bulbs soon clump up and need dividing every three years to keep them vigorous. It can be grown as a deterrent to aphids.

DILL An attractive hardy annual with feathery leaves which can be grown in a flower border or the wildflower garden. Sow in spring. It self-sows. Gather leaves while they are young. Leaves can be dried or frozen; seeds can be dried. A good plant for beneficial insects.

FENNEL An attractive perennial which does well in the flower border although it does self-sow. Sow seed in spring. Dry seed and freeze the leaves. Fennel attracts many beneficial insects.

LOVAGE A tall, rather coarse, perennial plant. It likes a moisture retentive soil, rich in organic material. Grow from seed or divide existing plants in spring. Freeze the leaves. Dry the leaves, seed, and root.

TOP TO BOTTOM *Borage* (Borago officinalis); *Chives* (Allium schoenoprasum) *and variegated lemon balm* (Melissa officinalis 'Variegata'); *Dill* (Anethum graveolens).

INDIVIDUAL HERBS

MARJORAM A perennial, of which some forms are tender, majoram likes a well-drained but rich soil. Sow or divide in spring. It does self-sow. Dry or freeze the leaves. It attracts bees and butterflies.

MINT A perennial, of which several varieties are attractive enough for the flower border. Plant in autumn or spring. It can be very invasive, but can be controlled by planting in a confined space such as a bottomless bucket sunk to its rim in soil. Store the leaves by drying or freezing. Mint can deter aphids and cabbage pests.

ROSEMARY A very attractive shrubby perennial which goes well in ornamental borders. Plant out rooted cuttings in spring or autumn in well-drained soil. Dry the leaves or whole sprigs. Rosemary can be used to repel moths.

SAGE A shrubby perennial which is suitable for the flower garden. It likes a well drained soil. Plant out rooted cuttings in spring or autumn. Pick the leaves before the flowers appear and dry. Sage can discourage household insects.

SORREL This perennial herb will tolerate light shade. Sow as seed in spring or divide roots in autumn. Freeze the leaves.

TARRAGON Hardy herbs. Russian tarragon can be sown from seed in spring, while the best tarragon, the French, is grown from root divisions in spring. French tarragon may need protecting from frosts. Dry or freeze the leaves.

THYME A perennial herb with many varieties. Take cuttings and plant out in light, well-drained soil in full sunlight. This is a good herb for planting on patios in surface cracks. Dry the leaves. Thyme attracts bees and is said to deter cabbage pests.

TOP TO BOTTOM *Fennel* (Foeniculum vulgare); *Rosemary* (Rosmarinus officinalis); *Lemon thyme* (Thymus x citriodorus).

ABOVE A *herb garden is a delightful setting in which to relax and work. The pungent aromas and the drowsy sound of bees can be very therapeutic, and it is worthwhile placing a seat in a strategic spot.*

CULTIVATION

~

Herbs generally like a well-drained soil but they also like a reasonably well-fed one. So prepare the ground by double digging and incorporating well rotted manure or compost. Heavy or wet soils should have gravel or sharp sand added to them. Most herbs come from chalky areas and prefer a pH just on the alkaline side of neutral, between 7 and 7.5, so acid soils should be adjusted accordingly. Make certain that the soil is completely weed free.

Sow or plant herbs in the spring. Keep weeded and do not allow the rampant ones,

such as the mints, to crowd the others. These can be kept in control by planting them in a bottomless bucket sunk in the soil.

Keep the garden weeded and remove the inevitable self-sown seedlings before they take over. Shear off plants that get too leggy and any that are turning to seed (unless, of course, the seed is the main purpose of the plant).

Many herbs can be harvested and dried for winter use. Hang them in bunches in a cool, airy position until they have dried completely then store in airtight containers. Alternatively, some plants can be frozen.

On the whole herbs are trouble free and present few problems.

8 THE ORNAMENTAL GARDEN

FLOWERING PLANTS PLAY AN important part in the organic garden. A well-stocked flower garden will attract a wide range of beneficial insects, which will help to combat the ravages of the more harmful ones.

In many respects, the same principles apply to the flower garden as to the vegetable garden. Provide a good soil, enriched with organic material, and avoid monocultures. Gardeners who specialize in one type of plant often find that when pests or diseases strike they do so disastrously, running through the whole stock with little chance of a natural cure being able to cope. For example, if you insist on growing nothing but roses you are inevitably going to have problems with greenfly. On the other hand, with mixed borders, a particular problem has less chance of gaining the upper hand. If it does, usually only one of many different types of plant is affected, something the gardener can live with. Besides, a mixed flower garden is more attractive.

BELOW We tend to think of ornamental gardens in terms of their bright floral display, but the foliage and shapes of vegetables can add a great deal to the overall picture.

~ PLANNING AND DESIGN ~

The organic flower garden *par excellence* is the cottage garden. These were rarely designed, but simply evolved into wonderful mixed displays of colors and textures. There was often no differentiation between vegetables, flowers, and fruit, so green beans could be found among the daisies, and cabbages with the dahlias.

BELOW *Annual plants give a wonderful touch of colourful spontaneity to a border, especially if the seed is scattered, rather than sown in rows. Here jostling poppies and foxgloves complement each other.*

OPPOSITE *Perennials around a pond can bring a deep sense of tranquillity, so valuable in a garden. Equally valuable is the pond itself, a mini ecosystem which encourages a remarkably diverse population of wildlife to the garden.*

ABOVE *Curved borders always look more interesting than straight ones. Here they enclose a huge diversity of annuals, perennials, and rock plants, as well as trees and shrubs. Normally, the greater the variety of plants, the healthier your garden will be.*

Many of the flowering plants were self-sowing annuals. These needed little care and certainly none of the cossetting that many modern bedding plants require. The perennials were tough plants which could look after themselves. If they were prone to pests and diseases, they tended to die out. So many of the old-fashioned flowers that have been handed down to us are the ones to look for and to grow. Fortunately, there are still many of them around. Also go for those plants that are attractive to bees and the range of beneficial insects. Avoid, on both counts, many of the modern cultivars that languish without regular attention to rid them of greenfly, or have no passing interest for beneficial insects.

The layout of flower gardens is very much an individual choice, although there are one or two basic principles. The first is that the garden is all the more interesting if you cannot see it all at once. Paths and borders twisting out of sight generate a sense of mystery. Straight edge borders are fine for formal plantings but tend to draw the eye to the far end, whereas the

hollows of a curved border hold the attention and the prominences stop the eye from moving off, so you pay more attention to what is growing there. Gentle sinuous curves look better than abrupt changes of direction.

Flowering plants always look best against a background, be it manmade, such as a wall, or natural, such as a hedge. Plants should generally be arranged with the shortest at the front and tallest at the back, but it is a good idea to pull a few of the taller ones forward to break up the symmetry or it will become boring.

Within the border, arrange the plants so that there is always something in flower. For example, plant asters so that they can take over from the earlier speedwells. Some plants, such as peonies, have arresting foliage in spring and again in autumn, as well as their period of flower. Trees and shrubs act as a permanent structure to the border, even in winter when the herbaceous plants have retired beneath the soil. They also provide interesting color and texture with their foliage as well as their flower.

PLANTING AND MAINTENANCE

The soil for ornamental borders should be prepared as carefully as that for vegetable plots. Unless you are only growing annuals the planting is likely to be permanent, or at least in place for a number of years. This makes it essential to remove all possible weeds and to prepare the ground thoroughly, adding as much organic material as possible. Trees and shrubs, particularly, need to have moisture-retentive material near their roots and a constant supply of nutrients. Organic material can be supplemented by slow-release organic fertilizers such as bone meal.

Plant perennials, trees, and shrubs either in the autumn or spring, the latter being best for cold areas. Most need to be planted to the same depth that they were in their pots or nursery bed. Trees and some shrubs need to be staked to prevent the roots from being rocked. It is only the lower third of the tree that needs staking; the rest should be left free to move in the wind.

Some herbaceous plants also need to be staked against the wind. Small sticks can be pushed into the ground close to the plant and their tops bent over and woven into a mesh when the plant is at about half its eventual height. The plant will then grow through the sticks and completely cover them with foliage. Another method is to put stakes in the ground and weave a cat's cradle of string between them, giving the same effect as the sticks. You can also buy special wire or plastic supports.

Mulch the borders to keep down weeds, help certain the moisture, and feed the soil. You can use grass clippings, or any of the other materials previously suggested. Remove dead flower heads for a succession of blooms. As the plants die back for winter, cut down all the old material and compost it. The tougher material can be shredded. During the winter, top-dress with well rotted manure or seed-free compost.

SUPPORTING SHRUBS

Many plants need some support, especially in gardens with exposed areas. Special supports can be purchased or they can be improvised from stakes and sticks. Net held horizontally between posts can be used for large plantings.

ANNUALS AND BIENNIALS

Many hardy species can be sown in the autumn so they start flowering earlier, the next spring.

BORAGE (*Borago officinalis*) Really a herb, borage makes a delightful annual which attracts bees and other beneficial insects. It has blue flowers, useful for adding to salads, from summer onward. Hardy.

CORNFLOWER (*Centaurea cyanus*) A popular garden plant which is useful for the wild garden as well as the borders. Useful for beneficial insects. The flowers are usually blue, but other colors can also be found. Flowers summer onward. Hardy.

FOXGLOVE (*Digitalis*) A biennial, this delightful cottage garden plant sows itself freely. It has the advantage of being both rabbit and deer proof. The flowers are a soft purple. It flowers from late spring onward. Hardy.

FRENCH MARIGOLDS (*Tagetes*) A very good plant for attracting beneficial insects to the garden. Often planted among vegetables. It flowers summer onward. Tender.

LOVE-IN-A-MIST (*Nigella*) A wonderful European cottage garden favorite, with blue or white buttercuplike flowers. It is one of the easiest plants to grow and self-sows. It flowers from late spring onward. Hardy.

MIGNONETTE (*Reseda odorata*) Grown for centuries in cottage gardens because of its wonderful, almost overpowering, scent. The flowers are yellow. It flowers from late summer onward. Hardy.

NASTURTIUM (*Tropaeolum majus*) A climbing plant with orange or yellow plants. The leaves can be used in salads. It deters whitefly and can be used to attract aphids away from other crops. It flowers from summer onward. Tender.

PHACELIA (*Phacelia*) One of the best plants for attracting beneficial insects to the garden. Plant close to the vegetable garden. The flowers are mainly various shades of blue. It flowers from late spring onward. Hardy.

French marigold (Tagetes patula)

Variegated nasturtium (Tropaeolum majus 'Alaska')

Snapdragons (Antirrhinum majus)

Tobacco plant (Nicotiana 'Crimson Rocket')

PINK (*Dianthus chinensis*) An old-fashioned plant for the front of a border, with pink, white, and red flowers. Modern forms are often quite brash. Some are scented. Flowers mid summer onward. Tender.

POACHED EGG FLOWER (*Limnanthes douglasii*) A delightful white and yellow flower for the front of the border. Very attractive to bees and other beneficial plants. It self-sows. Hardy.

SCABIOUS (*Scabiosa*) A plant much seen in cottage gardens, where it was appreciated not only for its delicate colors but because it attracts bees. Flowers late summer onwards. Tender.

SNAPDRAGON (*Antirrhinum majus*) A delightful old-fashioned plant. It was trouble free until the advent of antirrhinum rust fungus in the 1930's. It is now important to choose a rust-free strain. Flower colors are mixed. Flowers spring onward. Hardy.

SWEET PEA (*Lathyrus odoratus*) One of the best-loved of scented flowers. Beware, not all modern cultivars are scented. They are climbing plants. There is a wide range of colors. Hardy.

SWEET WILLIAM (*Dianthus barbatus*) Biennial. A cottage garden favourite with a delightful fragrance. Trouble free. Flowers are red, pink, and white. Early summer flowering. Hardy.

TOBACCO PLANT (*Nicotiana*) A plant with good flowers which have a particular strong perfume in the evening. They will self-sow. Flowering is from summer onward. Tender.

VIPER'S BUGLOSS (*Echium vulgare*) Also known as blueweed. Biennial. Bright blue flowers much loved by bees and other insects. Happy in dry soil. Flowers summer onward. Hardy.

WALLFLOWER (*Cheiranthus*) Biennial. An old-fashioned flower which no garden should be without. It has a wonderful scent. Generally trouble free but can suffer from club root so do not plant on soil in which cabbages have grown previously and resite each year. Various colors. Early summer flowering. Hardy.

~
PERENNIALS
~

ASTER (*Aster*) A good plant for the latter part of the season. There is a wide range of colors. Autumn asters can suffer from mildew but this can be alleviated by providing moisture retentive soil and good air circulation. They are very attractive to bees, butterflies, and beneficial insects. Rabbits tend to leave them alone. 1–5 ft. (30–150 cm).

BEE BALM (*Monarda didyma*) A very aromatic plant, also known as Oswego tea, which can be used for herbal teas. It is very attractive to bees. Can suffer from mildew if soil is allowed to dry out, so add plenty of organic material. The flowers are usually pink, red, or purple and appear in the summer. 3–4 ft. (90–120 cm).

BLACK-EYED SUSAN, CONEFLOWER (*Rudbeckia*) A genus of yellow daisies, usually with a black center, hence one of its names. Plants flower late in the season and dislike dry soil so add plenty of moisure retaining organic material. They are immune to rabbits and deer, but bees favor them. 2–4 ft. (60–120 cm).

CALAMINT (*Calamintha*) A low, bushy plant which flowers over a very long period. It has fragrant leaves and is much loved by bees and other beneficial insects. Plants like a light, well drained soil in full sun. The tiny flowers are either pink or white. 12–18 in. (30–45 cm).

CATNIP (*Nepeta cataria*) A floppy plant for the front of the border which has a haze of soft lavender or blue flowers. As its name suggests, cats love it, but deer and rabbits hate it. Bees also like it. It flowers throughout the summer and into autumn. It likes a well-drained soil. 1–3 ft. (30–90 cm).

CHRYSANTHEMUM (*Chrysanthemum*) This is one of the best-loved garden plants. Most flower later in the year and are useful for autumn color as well as for cut flowers. The flowers come in a very good range of colors, shapes, and sizes. They like a rich soil. The florist chrysanthemums are tender and need lifting and storing over winter. 1–3 ft. (30–90 cm).

Autumn aster (Aster novi-belgii 'Carnival')

Bergamot (Monarda didyma)

Cranesbill (Geranium himalayense)

COLUMBINE, GRANNY'S BONNETS (*Aquilegia*) A much-loved group of old cottage garden plants. The flowers have an airy delicacy about them. There is quite a range of colors. They are quite drought resistant. The soil should be light and well drained. Plants will take light shade and flower from mid spring into the summer. 30 in. (75 cm).

COREOPSIS (*Coreopsis*) Plants of this genus have stiff wiry stems which carry bright yellow or crimson daisies from summer well into autumn. They are quite drought resistant and will grow in any soil. They are attractive to a range of beneficial insects, including bees. 2 ft. (60 cm).

DEADNETTLE (*Lamium*) The deadnettle is a very good plant to use in the garden, both because plants form a dense mat which acts as a ground cover and also because they are rarely out of flower. The main varieties have pink flowers. Rabbits ignore them. They will grow in any soil. 12 in. (30 cm).

ELEPHANT'S EAR (*Bergenia*) A valuable group of plants with large glossy leaves which form a very good evergreen ground cover. They have nicely contrasting pink or white spikes of flowers in spring. They are useful as they will grow in shade as well as sun and will survive in quite dry conditions. Rabbits dislike them. 1–2 ft. (30–60 cm).

GERANIUM (*Geranium*) This is the hardy geranium, as opposed to the pelargonium. It is one of the mainstays of any garden, with over 200 species and varieties to choose from. Plants are generally trouble free and many will grow in shade as well as in sun. Some make excellent ground cover. They are reasonably resistant to drought and are not eaten by rabbits or deer. Colors vary from white and pink to blue and purple. Various varieties flower from mid spring to late autumn. 6 in.–3 ft. (15–90 cm).

GOAT'S BEARD (*Astilbe*) This plant carries feathery heads of bright flowers in the latter part of summer. These vary in color from cream, through pink to red. A moist, organic-rich soil is required and plants do particularly well beside water. They are useful for growing in shade. They tend to be both deer and rabbit proof. 2–4 ft. (60–120 cm).

GLOBE THISTLE (*Echinops*) The flowers of this genus are carried in intriguing spheres, either blue or white in color. They flower in summer. Bees absolutely adore them. The foliage is prickly. They will grown on light soils and are rabbit proof. 4–6 ft. (120–180 cm).

HOSTA, PLAINTAIN LILY (*Hosta*) Although it produces flowers in the autumn, this plant is mainly grown for its attractive foliage. It can form dense colonies, making excellent ground cover. Slugs love the leaves, but rabbits and deer ignore them. These versatile plants will grow in a range of soils, although preferring an organic-rich one, and in either sun or shade. 1–3 ft. (30–90 cm).

ICE PLANT, STONECROP (*Sedum*) A valuable plant for the autumn scene which is always covered with bees and butterflies as well as other beneficial insects. The flower heads vary from pink to red and turn brown in late autumn. The plants like a well-drained soil, preferably rich in organic material. 9–18 in. (23–45 cm).

IRIS (*Iris*) No garden would be complete without irises. Some species prefer a well-drained position while other are happier in moist soil or even in water. The flowers cover a wide range of colors, including almost black. Some flower in the depths of winter, others in summer. Rabbits or deer leave them alone. 12–48 in. (30–120 cm).

JAPANESE ANEMONE (*Anemone x hybrida*) A valuable group of late-flowering plants. The flowers have a purity about them and are white or pink. They will grow in a range of soils but do not like to be too dry. They will grow in light shade. Rabbits dislike them.

KNAPWEED (*Centaurea*) A genus related to the thistles, but these are not thugs. The flowers are usually rose-purple although some are yellow. They flower from spring until autumn and are good bee plants. 2–5 ft. (60–150 cm).

LEOPARD'S BANE (*Doronicum*) This carries bright yellow daisy-type flowers in the early spring and does much to brighten up the scene, especially in shady corners. Plants are tolerant of a range of soils. They provide early sustenance for bees and other beneficial insects, while rabbits do not seem to like them. 18–36 in. (45–90 cm).

MILKWEED, BUTTERFLY WEED (*Asclepias*) An attractive plant which likes a warm position and light soil. The flowers are pink or orange, appearing from summer into autumn. Bees love them and they are host to parasites for the codling moth so they are worth planting near apple and apricot trees. 18–36 in. (45–90 cm).

PEONY (*Paeonia*) A valuable plant, as both the spring and autumn foliage is very attractive and it bears superb flowers in spring and early summer. Many of the double flowers can become very heavy and floppy when filled with rain. The color varies from white and yellow, through pink and red. Rabbits and deer do not eat them. 1–3 ft. (30–90 cm).

Ice plant (Sedum spectabile)

Peony (Paeonia)

Red Hot Poker (Kniphofia)

PURPLE CONE FLOWER (*Echinacea*) A wonderful plant which produces large cartwheel daisies with purple petals. These appear in late summer and autumn, and are always covered with bees and butterflies. It likes a rich, but well drained soil. 4 ft. (120 cm).

PURPLE LOOSESTRIFE (*Lythrum*) A moisture-loving plant which likes an organic-rich soil and is good for planting near water. The purple spikes of flowers appear in summer. They are good plants for attracting bees. 3–4 ft. (90–120 cm).

RED HOT POKER (*Kniphofia*) Valuable for its upright shape and unique flower head. Colors range form hot yellows and reds to cooler lemons and greens. Plants flower from summer through to autumn. They can make dense ground cover and rabbits and deer do not like them. Give them a rich, free-draining soil. 2–7 ft. (60–200 cm).

SEA HOLLY (*Eryngium maritimum*) An attractive European prickly plant, often with steely blue leaves and flower heads. The flowers appear in summer and are good for drying. Bees are very much attracted to them, but rabbits and deer leave them alone. Plants like a free-draining soil. 2–6 ft. (30–180 cm).

SNEEZEWEED (*Helenium*) A good genus of garden plants with daisy-type flowers which appear from mid summer onward. The colors are mainly yellows and browns. Bees love them. They are versatile and will grow on almost any type of soil. 2–5 ft. (60–150 cm).

SPEEDWELL (*Veronica*) A large genus loved for its blue flowers although there are also some white and pink-flowered forms. Plants bloom from early summer through to the autumn. They like a well-drained soil and most are reasonably drought proof. Bees and other beneficial insects love them. 1–6 ft. (30–180 cm).

SPURGE (*Euphorbia*) An enormous family of ornamental plants which are grown for their ornamental bracts, the flowers being insignificant. The caper spurge (*E. lathyrus*) deters moles while deer and rabbits do not like any of them. They will grow in any fertile soil and will take both sun and shade. 1–6ft (30–180 cm).

~
TREES AND SHRUBS
~

BARBERRY (*Berberis*) A genus of shrubs, mainly with prickly foliage which makes them good for informal hedges. Grown for both leaf (spring and autumn) and flower colors, and often for colorful fruit. Many are evergreen. The flowers are attractive to bees. They will grow on most soils, in full sun or light shade. Up to 10 ft. (3 m).

BIRCH (*Betula*) This tree is grown mainly for its attractive bark. The leaves have a good autumn color. Fruit and flowers are of little significance. It will grow on a wide range of soil, especially light ones, but prefers full sun. It self-sows. Up to 40 ft. (12 m).

BUTTERFLY BUSH (*Buddleja*) This attractive bush, also called budoleja, is grown for its flowers, which are extremely attractive to butterflies and other insects. The flower color varies from lavender to red, white and yellow. The fruit and autumn foliage are insignificant. It needs severe pruning each spring and is best in a sunny position in a light soil. Up to 13 ft. (4 m).

CAMELLIA (*Camellia*) A very popular genus of shrubs grown for their spring flowers and glossy, evergreen leaves. The flowers vary from white to pink and red; insignificant fruit. Buds can suffer from frosts so it is best to plant this shrub away from early morning sun which thaws it out too quickly. It must have an acid soil. Up to 20 ft. (6 m).

COTONEASTER (*Cotoneaster*) This genus includes a wide range of species, grown mainly for their autumn berries and also for their small white flowers which are of great interest to bees and many beneficial insects. They flower from late spring to early summer. Most are evergreen, but there are a few deciduous ones. They will tolerate a wide range of soils, including dry ones. Up to 20 ft. (6 m).

Camellia (Camellia japonica).

Honeysuckle (Lonerica × Americana).

Lavender (Lavandula angustifolia 'Hidcote')

FUCHSIA (*Fuchsia*) A genus with a few species and a large number of cultivars, mainly grown for their pendulous flowers although a few also have attractive foliage. They flower from early summer onward. Most are tender and even the hardy varieties can be cut to the ground by frosts. The fruit is insignificant. They like a wide range of soils as long as they are well drained. Up to 6 ft. (180 cm).

HONEYSUCKLE (*Lonicera*) A big group of climbing plants and shrubs, many of which bear highly fragrant flowers. They are valuable for attracting beneficial insects, but they can also attract aphids. They flower from spring onward and there are three species which flower in winter. They have attractive fruit. Honeysuckle will grow on most soils in full sun to light shade. Up to 20 ft. (6 m).

HYDRANGEA (*Hydrangea*) A large genus of shrubs noted for their large colorful flower heads. Colors include white, blue, pink, and red. They appear in bloom from mid summer onward. The dried flower heads can be attractive. Plants may be a bit tender and should be planted in a sheltered position; they dislike a dry soil. Up to 13 ft. (4 m).

IVY (*Hedera*) A climbing plant which flowers in late autumn and provides nectar for a large number of beneficial insects. Ivy is grown mainly for the evergreen leaves, which are variegated in many species. The black berries that appear in winter can also be attractive. It will climb up to 40 ft. (12 m), but can also be grown as ground cover or as shrubs.

JASMINE (*Jasminum*) A highly scented shrub which flowers in the summer. The flowers are either white, pink, or yellow. There is one form, J. *nudiflorum*, which flowers in mid winter. The fruit is insignificant. Jasmine will grow on any soil, even poor ones. Up to 10 ft. (3 m).

LAVENDER (*Lavandula*) A group of aromatic shrubs which flower during summer. The color varies from lavender and blue to purple. The shrubs are wonderfully fragrant and the flowers are good for drying. Lavender must have a light, well-drained soil and a sunny position. Up to 3 ft. (90 cm).

MAPLE (*Acer*) A very interesting group of trees, grown for the color of their leaves, both in spring and autumn, and for the color of their bark Their fruiting "keys" can be attractive. Maples will grow on a wide range of soils in light shade or sun. The flowers and fruit are generally insignificant. Up to 60 ft. (18 m).

MOUNTAIN ASH, ROWAN (*Sorbus aucuparia*) A delightful group of trees suitable for the small garden. They have clusters of white flowers in spring and red, white or yellow berries in the autumn. Mountain ashes will grow on any soil and in either full sun or light shade. 20–30 ft. (6–9 m).

RHODODENDRON, AZALEA (*Rhododendron*) An enormous genus of shrubs and trees bearing flowers mainly in the spring. The flowers come in a wide range of colors; the fruit is insignificant. They are mainly evergreen but some azaleas are deciduous. They dislike alkaline soils and prefer light shade. Up to 20 ft. (6 m).

ROSEMARY (*Rosmarinus*) A shrub with aromatic evergreen leaves and small, pale-blue flowers which appear over a very long period. Insignificant in seed. Rosemary must have a well-drained soil in a sunny position and should be planted near a path where it can be touched for its fragrance. Up to 4 ft. (120 cm).

Japanese maple (Acer palmatum dissectum)

Mountain ash (Sorbus aucuparia) in fruit.

Azaleas (Rhododendron)

Rose (Rosa mundi)

Viburnum (Viburnum betulifolium) *in fruit.*

ROSE (*Rosa*) An enormous genus of shrubs and climbers which flower from spring onward in a wide range of colors. Many have very decorative hips. The species and many of the old-fashioned varieties are less prone to disease than many of the modern hybrids. Avoid planting as a monoculture but mix with other plants. Roses need fertile soil with plenty of organic material. Up to 20 ft. (6 m).

VIBURNUM (*Viburnum*) A delightful group of deciduous and evergreen plants, many of which are fragrant. Most flower in spring, but there are some winter-flowering species. Many are very attractive in fruit. They are trouble-free plants for most soils. Up to 16 ft. (5 m).

WILLOW (*Salix*) A large group of deciduous shrubs and trees grown for their foliage and spring flowers. They are thirsty plants and prefer a moist position. They are very good for planting in wet soil to help dry it out. Many benefit from hard pruning each year. Up to 40 ft. (12 m).

YEW (*Taxus*) In spite of its appearance the yew is not a conifer. It bears red fruit (which are poisonous) in summer. The early spring flowers are insignificant. Yews are mainly grown for their evergreen foliage, either green or golden, and their architectural qualities. Any soil. Up to 30 ft. (9 m).

9 WILDLIFE IN THE GARDEN

HERE ARE MANY REASONS for encouraging wildlife in the garden. First, there is the sheer pleasure of seeing it around. There cannot be a gardener who does not enjoy the sound of birdsong or the sight of a butterfly as he or she works. One marvellous insect in the garden is the bee, which provides both honey and wax. Until relatively recently man has always worked close to nature. He is now gravely in danger of losing this contact, much to both his disadvantage and that of the natural world.

With the loss of natural habitats, due to a number of causes, any extra which you can supply means that a few creatures are saved. A small pond, for example, can support a wide variety of wildlife. Even the trees and shrubs of a garden will encourage a surprising number of birds, insects, and even mammals to the area. Without due care it can be the baddies that rise to the top, so it is important to create habitats for these animals that prey on what we consider to be pests. Frogs, for example, will help keep the slug population down.

OPPOSITE *To most people, butterflies are one of the most welcome signs of wildlife in a garden. Here two small tortoiseshells bask on a* Sedum spectabile.

RIGHT *If you have the time and the space, a beehive can be a wonderful asset in the organic garden. But you must have experience in apiary before going ahead with installing one.*

PLANNING FOR WILDLIFE

Man can provide two basic things for wildlife: shelter and food. Shelter is no more than making available a range of differing habitats. For example, birds like to roost and nest in trees and shrubs, many preferring denser foliage in which they can hide. While choosing trees and shrubs this is something you can bear in mind, so that you provide a good mixture, some with evergreen foliage which will give more protection in winter. Similarly, you can supplement their diet by choosing plants with plenty of berries. Do not be in a hurry to tidy up old herbaceous plants in the autumn as many dying stems carry seed heads and quantities of insects, which are food to many birds.

Mammals choose a variety of habitats and a few crevices left in the rock garden or around a pool will not go amiss. Nor will a few patches of long grass where a lot of beneficial insects will overwinter.

BELOW Dragonflies seem to appear in myriad sizes and colors as soon as a pond has been dug. They are wonderful insects to have in the garden.

SEEDING PLANTS FOR BIRDS AND MAMMALS

- Autumn asters (*Aster*)
- Birch (*Betula*)
- Campion (*Silene*)
- Chickweed (*Stellaria*)
- Chrysanthemum (*Chrysanthemum*)
- Clover (*Trifolium*)
- Cuckoo pint (*Arum maculatum*) (poisonous)
- Dandelion (*Taraxacum*)
- Foxglove (*Digitalis*) (poisonous)
- Globe thistle (*Echinops*)
- Goldenrod (*Solidago*)
- Grasses (various)
- Groundsel (*Senecio*)
- Knapweed (*Centaurea*)
- Peony (*Paeonia*)
- Teasel (*Dipsacus*)
- Thistle (*Cirsium*)
- Verbena (*Verbena*)
- Violet (*Viola*)

FRUITING TREES AND SHRUBS FOR BIRDS AND MAMMALS

- Apples (*Malus*)
- Barberry (*Berberis*)
- Beech (*Fagus*)
- Bramble, Blackberry (*Rubus*)
- Cherry (*Prunus*)
- Cotoneaster (*Cotoneaster*)
- Daphne (*Daphne*)
- Elder (*Sambucus*)
- Firethorn (*Pyracantha*)
- Hawthorn (*Crataegus monogyna*)
- Hazel (*Corylus*)
- Holly (*Ilex*)
- Honeysuckle (*Lonicera*)
- Ivy (*Hedera*)
- Mountain ash, rowan (*Sorbus aucuparia*)
- Rose (*Rosa*)
- Viburnum (*Viburnum*)
- Yew (*Taxus*) (poisonous to humans)

Plants that will attract beneficial insects to the garden have already been mentioned in the sections on herbs, annuals and perennials. They not only provide nourishment for beneficial insects, but also for foraging bees and any gardener who wants to gather his own honey would do well to plant as many of these as possible.

Another side to wildlife is wildflowers. More and more gardeners are finding space for at least a few of their native flora. You should never remove these from the countryside (unless they are in immediate danger of being bulldozed), but most are available as seed from the many seed merchants who now specialize in them. Wildflowers are not as brash or bold as many of the garden varieties, but they usually have a wonderful simplicity which makes them beautiful in their own right. Another significant advantage of growing them is that they attract native insects, many of which are beneficial.

ABOVE *Wildlife is not restricted to animals; wild flowers are just as much part of the natural scene. Having them in the flower beds helps to attract native insects, which are often the ones on the gardener's side.*

95

 # LAWNS, PATHS, AND PATIOS

S O FAR, THIS BOOK HAS been about the beds and borders in which vegetables, ornamentals, and other plants are grown. There are also the areas in between to consider. Nearly every garden has paths, and often lawns and paved areas.

BELOW *Essentially, lawns are visually quiet areas which break up the hurly-burly of the borders. Without these "islands" the eye is likely to find the garden too busy.*

PAVED AREAS

Paved areas, as such, have little to do with organic gardening, but there are a few implications. If patios and paths are laid from concrete slabs or bricks, there may well be gaps between individual units. Weeds make the most of any opportunities and are likely to grow in these cracks. It is not easy to remove them from this position and many gardeners resort to using weed killers, often persistent ones to prevent re-emergence. However, chemicals can be avoided with some forethought.

Make sure, before any slabs are laid, that all perennial weeds have been removed. Putting a sheet of black polyethylene over the whole area and bedding the slabs on top of this will prevent anything growing up from the soil. However, dust and detritus will collect in the gaps, providing enough nourishment for weeds to move in. You can prevent this by filling in the gaps between the slabs or bricks with cement.

Many gardeners like to put plants on a patio. One way is to leave out the occasional slab and plant here. Dig out the soil and dig in a good quantity of organic material as it may be some years before it is redug, especially if shrubs are planted. Similarly, if you construct raised beds around the edge of the paved area, include a good layer of well-rotted manure or compost in the bottom of each.

ABOVE RIGHT *Paths are valuable for linking different areas of the garden, both physically and visually. Among the wide range of materials that can be used, gravel is attractive and relatively cheap, but can get scattered around and picked up on muddy boots.*

RIGHT *Within paved areas, suitable plants are often placed in the gaps between slabs. But unless regularly maintained, weeds will take them over and ruin the effect.*

~ LAWNS ~

Unlike paved areas, lawns and grass paths are growing organisms and need to be treated as such to perform of their best. Many gardeners pour more chemicals in the way of fertilizers, and weed and moss killers, onto their lawns than they do onto the rest of the garden. It is just as important to avoid doing this here as anywhere else. You do not eat the grass, but chemicals will find their way into other parts of the garden through grass clippings or leaching into the soil. Besides, think what it costs.

Many of the problems that the chemicals are intended to solve can be prevented in the first place. The weed killers are needed because too many weeds were left in the soil, and the moss killers are required because the lawn is damp enough to support mosses. With good initial preparation both these problems can be reduced.

Before laying a lawn, make sure that you have removed all perennial weeds from the site. Leave it for a while and then remove any that reappear. Add drainage material to the soil to lighten it and install a drainage system if water is lying on the surface.

Once the lawn is in existence, regular mowing will help to reduce the number of

THE RIGHT GRASS FOR YOUR LAWN

Choose the seed with which you sow your lawn and paths with care. Areas that do not take much traffic can be sown with a mixture of fine grasses including the bents and the fescues. These will give a more velvety appearance. If the area is to take heavy traffic, on a path or where children play, for example, the mixture should include hard-wearing types such as the ryegrasses.

OPPOSITE *Patios or terraces are ideal places for creating container gardens, using pots and tubs. They can, as here, involve decorative plants or herbs and even vegetables.*

BELOW *Lawns need not be any less organic than the vegetable garden. It is without doubt the most valuable part of a garden and constant supervision is the key to success.*

ABOVE *Lawns complement flower borders well, but must be kept mown; otherwise, the untidy long grass will adversely affect the garden's whole appearance. Plants that flop over it can create bald patches that will need resowing.*

perennial weeds that may appear. Cut out those that still survive with a knife. Regularly remove any thatch which appears on the lawn by raking it vigorously. Aerate the lawn by spiking it, either with a special tool or a fork. Both these operations allow air to circulate around the grasses and prevent them from becoming too damp, encouraging mosses.

Mow frequently so that the clippings are short. These can be left to be recycled into the soil, feeding it. Do not leave longer clippings on the lawn as those will kill off the underlying grass.

Some areas of lawn can be left as a wilder area in which to grow bulbs such as daffodils (*Narcissus*). Cut the grass once the bulbs' leaves have died down.

11 ORGANIC CONTAINERS

CONTAINER GARDENING HAS increased a great deal in recent years, mainly in the area of decorative plants. However, the imaginative gardener can also grow vegetables, herbs, and even fruit by this method.

Containers have several advantages. You can have a sequence of attractive plants on display when they are at their best and remove them when they begin to flag. This means that high profile areas such as patios can always look their best. You can grow tender plants and overwinter them by taking the container inside. People who have little space can create an attractive environment and possibly even grow a few vegetables. Plants which are grown in containers can be given more individual attention and arranged in attractive groups.

RIGHT *Containers can greatly enliven the bare sweep of wooden decks. A wide range of ornamental plants can be grown, from annuals, as here, to perennials and shrubs.*

RIGHT A *wonderful mixture of bright annuals. It is essential to have a good moisture-retaining compost to get such vigorous growth. If you make your own, use plenty of organic material and supplement it with a liquid feed at least once every two weeks.*

THE CONTAINERS

Anything which will hold soil can be used as a ~ontainer for plants. The extreme of this is the plastic bag, which manifests itself as the ubiquitous growing bag. While this type of container is very useful, you can do a little better for plants which are to be part of the decorative scene in the garden. Garden centers now provide a large range of ceramic and plastic containers. They should always have a drainage hole or holes in the bottom.

Nearly all the potting composts that you are likely to buy will contain non-organic fertilizers. The only way to avoid this is to make up your own compost, mixing one-third good loam (old stacked turfs are fine for this),

one third sharp sand or fine gravel, and one-third sieved leaf mold or coir fiber. This last ingredient can be one sixth leaf mold or coir and one sixth well-rotted manure or compost, which will give the compost some nutritional value. For composts which are likely to stay in the container for some time a handful of dried blood, fish, or bone meal will act as a slow-release fertilizer.

Put the container in its final position before filling it with compost. First put in a layer of stones to help with drainage and then the compost. Do not compress too much, just tamp down lightly. The soil should be damp when the plants are put in and then watered immediately. Never let the containers dry out, which may mean watering every day, especially if you use terracotta pots.

HERBS FOR CONTAINERS

- Basil (*Ocimum basilicum*)
- Bay (*Laurus nobilis*)
- Chervil (*Anthriscus cerefolium*)
- Chives (*Allium schoenoprasum*)
- Coriander (*Coriandrum sativum*)
- Marjoram (*Origanum*)
- Mint (*Mentha*)
- Parsley (*Petroselinum crispum*)
- Rosemary (*Rosmarinus officinalis*)
- Sage (*Salvia officinalis*)
- Tarragon (*Artemisia dracunculus*)
- Thyme (*Thymus*)

RIGHT *An ideal way to grow herbs is to plant them in pots, which can be placed on a patio, close to the kitchen door. This renders them convenient to pick as well as invitingly available to run your fingers through every time you pass.*

ABOVE *Secure window boxes make ideal places to grow a range of plants, especially herbs in kitchen boxes. Against walls, by windows, boxes provide a form of protection against weather.*

TYPES OF CONTAINER

Containers need not be confined to those standing on the ground. You can also use hanging baskets and window boxes to grow a wide range of plants. A kitchen windowsill is a good place for a box of herbs. You can place window boxes on balconies, and climbing vegetables such as green beans or zucchini can grow up the railings. As long as it is kept well pruned, a grape vine could be grown in a similar way.

THE PLANTS

A wide range of decorative plants can be grown. This is not restricted to annuals but can include bulbs, perennials, shrubs, and even small trees. Ferns are especially good for shady areas. Try to include plants which will attract beneficial insects (see sections on annuals and perennials).

A surprising number of vegetables can be grown in containers. Green beans, supported on poles or strings, can make a very decorative feature. Tomatoes are among the most popular subjects, but you can also grow other salad crops such as lettuce and radishes.

Herbs do very well in containers and can be left handy near the kitchen door. In winter, the pot can be brought indoors.

Fruit, especially strawberries, make a welcome addition to any patio. They may have to be covered in net to prevent losses to birds.

LEFT *There is no reason why vegetables cannot be grown in containers as long as they are big enough. This old half barrel, containing a well-rotted compost, is producing a fine crop of carrots.*

FRUIT IN CONTAINERS

Strawberries are among the most popular fruits for planting in single pots. Special containers, which will need net covers as the fruit ripens, allow several plants to grow in a stack.

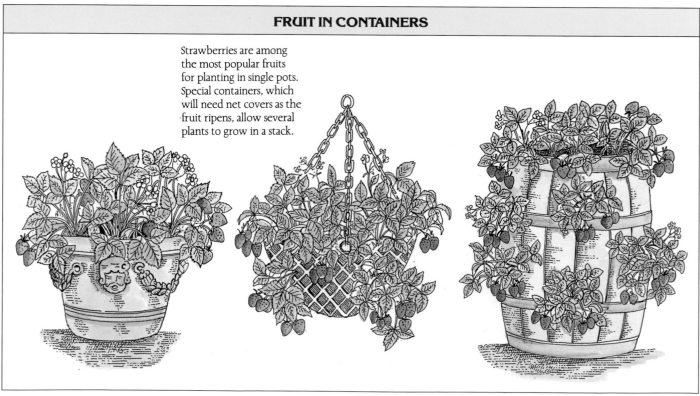

THE ORGANIC GREENHOUSE

A GREENHOUSE IS NOT essential, but it does widen the gardener's scope. As well as being able to grow plants which are too tender to overwinter outside, it allows you to produce young plants and vegetable crops earlier. It also provides a warm refuge for the gardener on a winter's day.

BELOW *Organic principles should be as prevalent in conservatories and greenhouses as in the outdoors. Unfortunately, conditions are not only conducive to growing plants, but also to harboring insects – so pay special attention.*

GREENHOUSE SHAPES

There is a wide range of different shapes and sizes of greenhouse available as well as a choice between wood and aluminum frames, and glass and plastic windows. The differences between materials is discussed in the text.

Conservatory

Circular

Traditional

THE CHOICE OF MATERIALS

The two main structural materials for greenhouses are wood and aluminum. Wooden greenhouses are marginally warmer than metal and easier to add to or modify. They need quite a bit of maintenance, especially to prevent them from rotting, but they generally look more attractive in the garden. Aluminum houses are a bit colder, but they require virtually no maintenance. Cheaper ones can flex in high winds so that the glass falls out.

The window panels can be either the traditional glass or modern plastics. The latter are much lighter in weight, but tend to scratch easily, reducing light transmission.

GREENHOUSES

A wide range of both ornamental and edible crops can be grown under glass. Because the greenhouse can be heated, you can bring seedlings on in advance of those in the open and plant them out once frosts have passed. You can also use it for growing pot plants, either for the house or for decorating the greenhouse itself.

Another important aspect is that you can grow a wide range of early vegetables, either in beds in the greenhouse or in growing bags. Early salad vegetables are especially welcome.

RIGHT *Greenhouses can be used to grow early crops, like lettuce, or those that need more warmth, like tomatoes. They can also be used to cultivate ornamental plants, either to be displayed for good in the greenhouse or taken into the house when in flower. The warm environment is also useful for raising bedding and other seedlings.*

PLANTING MEDIUM

Crops can be grown either directly in a bed in the border or in containers of some sort. As with the open garden it is a good idea to rotate crops under glass. However, this is not always possible, so the alternative is to change the soil. Soil can become sick with constantly growing tomatoes, for example, and the only way to keep producing good crops is to dig out all the soil from the beds each year and replace it with fresh. An alternative is to grow crops in growing bags which you change each season.

Any greenhouse soil should be high in organic materials to hold the moisture and help feed the plants. Bought growing bags are likely to contain chemical fertilizers, so it may be a good idea to make up your own compost using the formula given for containers on page 102.

Once the plants are growing they will need copious amounts of water. This may well lead to nutrients leaching and so you will need to give liquid feeds at two-week intervals.

HEATING

There are several ways of heating a greenhouse. The most popular is with an electric heater. Although electricity is relatively expensive it is possible, using thermostats, to have it on only when it is necessary. This means that the bills are kept to a minimum. Kerosene heaters are also popular, but they produce a lot of water vapor which can encourage damping off and other rot in plants. Insulating the greenhouse with sheets of bubble plastic will help to retain heat and at the same time will keep bills low.

BELOW *Greenhouse architecture is not restricted to the traditional cuboid model. Exciting new designs, well suited to the modern garden, will function just as well, given adequate ventilation.*

PESTS AND DISEASES

A greenhouse not only provides a good environment for growing plants, but also one that pests and diseases appreciate. The artificial atmosphere is conducive to far more pests than you normally find in the garden.

As in the open, good housekeeping and a vigilant eye can help a great deal. Healthy, vigorous plants are less likely to succumb to pests and diseases. If you remove rotting vegetation, dying leaves, and other pieces of detritus, there are fewer hiding and breeding places for the pests. Air circulation is important and this can be helped by good ventilation and the use of electric heaters which include fans.

Even when there are pests present there is no need to reach for the spray gun. Many can be controlled by using sticky yellow panels which attract and then trap the insects. In recent years there has been a breakthough in biological control and you can now buy insects which prey on specific pests. Once these are released into the greenhouse they kill off the pest. Most of the common pests can now be controlled in this way.

COLD FRAMES

If space or budget is limited, most things that are undertaken in a greenhouse can be done in a cold frame. This is a much lower structure which is much easier to keep warm as you can completely cover it with an old blanket or rug in cold weather. As with greenhouses, cold frames can be made either of aluminum or wood, with the same advantages and disadvantages applying.

RIGHT *Scrap or cheap materials can be used to construct a coldframe which is a fairly easy task. Plastic makes a suitable cover, but will need replacing after a couple of years.*

COLD FRAMES

Cold frames are far cheaper to buy and run than greenhouses, and serve the gardener just as well for most functions. Because of their small volume they can become very hot, so make sure to keep them properly ventilated and keep them shaded from direct sunlight during sunny weather.

BIBLIOGRAPHY

Ball, Jeff, *Rodale's Garden Problem Solver*, 1988.

Bird, Richard, *Companion Planting*, 1990.

Bradley, Fern Marshall and Ellis, Barbara W., *Rodale's All-New Encyclopedia of Organic Gardening*, 1992.

Carr, Anna, *Good Neighbours: Companion Planting for Gardeners*, 1985.

Cox, Jeff, *How to Grow Vegetables Organically*, 1988.

Hamilton, Geoff, *Successful Organic Gardening*, 1987.

Hills, Lawrence D., *Grow You Own Fruit and Vegetables*, 1971.

Lloyd, Christopher and Bird, Richard, *Cottage Gardening*, 1990.

Schulz, Warren, *The Chemical-free Lawn*, 1989.

Smith, Miranda and Carr, Anna, *Rodale's Garden Insect, Disease and Weed Identification Guide*, 1988.

Yepsen, Roger B., Jr, *The Encyclopedia of Natural Insect and Disease Control*, 1984.

SOCIETIES AND OTHER USEFUL ADDRESSES

American Horticultural Society, 7931 East Boulevard Drive, Alexandria, VA 22308, USA.

Biological Urban Gardening Services, PO Box 76, Citrus Heights, CA 95611, USA.

Canadian Organic Growers, PO Box 6408, Station J, Ottawa, ON K2A 3Y6, Canada.

Canadian Wildflower Society, 75 Ternhill Crescent, North York, ON M3C 2E4, Canada.

Cottage Garden Society, 5 Nixon Close, Thornhill, Dewsbury, W Yorks WF12 0JA, UK.

Henry Doubleday Research Association, Ryton-on-Dunsmore, Coventry CV8 3LG, UK.

Herb Society, 77 Peter Street, London SW1 2EZ, UK.

Herb Society of America, 9019 Kirtland Chardon Rd, Mentor, OH 44060, USA.

National Vegetable Association, 29 Revidge Road, Blackburn, Lancashire BB2 6JB, UK.

National Wildflower Research Centre, 2600 Fm 973 North, Austin, TX 78716-3172, USA.

Royal Horticultural Society, Vincent Square, London SW1P 2PE, UK.

Soil Association, 86 Colston Street, Bristol BS1 5BB, UK.

INDEX

PICTURE CREDITS

Quintet Publishing would like to thank the following for supplying the photographs used in this book:

Key: t=top, b=bottom, r=right, m=middle, l=left

2, 5 Harry Smith Collection; 7 John Glover; 8 John Ward/Unicorn Stock Photos; 9 Lance Beeny; 10 Dwight Kuhn; 11, 12, 13 John Glover; 14 Harry Smith Collection; 16 John Glover; 18 Marcus Schneck; 20 Grand Union; 24, 26 Harry Smith Collection; 27 Marcus Schneck; 30 Heather Angel; 32 John Glover; 34 (l) Harry Smith Collection; 35 Wildlife Matters; 36 Dede Gilman/Unicorn Stock Photos; 38 (r) Harry Smith Collection; 39 (r) Kimberley Burnham, (l) Marcus Schneck; 44 Heather Angel; 41, 42, 43, 49, 50, 51 (tl, br) Harry Smith Collection; 51 (tr) Marcus Schneck; 52 (l) John Glover, (m, r) Harry Smith Collection; 53 (l, r) Harry Smith Collection, (m) Jim Riddle/Unicorn Stock Photos; 54 (l) William H. Allen Jr, (m) Martha McBride/Unicorn Stock Photos, (r) Dwight Kuhn; 55 (l) Betts Anderson Builly, (m) Harry Smith Collection, (r) Marcus Schneck; 56 (l) Marcus Schneck, (r) Harry Smith Collection; 57 (l) Harry Smith Collection, (m) John Glover, (r) Martha McBride/Unicorn Stock Photos; 58 (l) Aneal Vohra/ Unicorn Stock Photos, (m) Harry Smith Collection, (r) Dwight Kuhn; 59 (l) Harry Smith Collection, (m) Betts Anderson/Unicorn Stock Photos, (r) Marcus Schneck; 60 (l, m) Harry Smith Collection, (r) Marcus Schneck; 61 (l) Dwight Kuhn, (m) John Glover, (r) Harry Smith Collection; 62 (l) Martha McBride/Unicorn Stock Photos, (m) John Glover, (r) Charles Schmidt/Unicorn Stock Photos; 63 (l) Harry Smith Collection, (m) Dwight Kuhn, (r) Martha McBride, Eric Bendt; 64 Harry Smith Collection; 65 John Glover; 67 Heather Angel; 69 Harry Smith Collection; 70, 71, 72 Heather Angel; 74 Harry Smith Collection; 75 (t) Harry Smith Collection, (m, b) Heather Angel; 76 Heather Angel; 77, 78 Harry Smith Collection; 79 Heather Angel; 80 John Glover; 81 (t) Harry Smith Collection; 81 (b) Heather Angel; 84, 85 (t, b), 86 Harry Smith Collection; 87, 88 Heather Angel; 89 John Glover; 90, 91 Heather Angel; 92 John Glover; 93 Harry Smith Collection; 94 Heather Angel; 95 Harry Smith Collection; 96, 97 (t) John Glover; 97 (b), 98 Heather Angel; 99 John Glover; 100, 101 Harry Smith Collection; 102 Heather Angel; 103, 104 Harry Smith Collection; 107 John Glover; 108 Harry Smith Collection; 109 Marcus Schneck.